France

French people, especially their leaders, are known for having distinctive ideas about their economic system, political and educational institutions and society. The Gaullist era marked the culmination of French 'exceptionalism' in the areas of economic protection, state-directed enterprise, elitist power structure and a foreign policy of grandeur. Thirty years later, all these aspects of French life are changing, bringing France into line with other European, and indeed international, standards of economic, political and cultural behaviour.

In this book, John Girling provides an informative and stimulating overview of French life in a climate of globalization and European integration. He critically examines the residual values of grandeur and elitism in the administrative, political and economic leadership of contemporary France and evaluates their changing profiles in the areas of education, domestic and foreign policy. Moreover, he analyses current political practice in the absence of major ideologies, the continuing scope for economic-political collusion nationally and in local government as well as the countervailing force of 'civil society' at a time of popular disillusionment with politics. Finally, the book addresses the question of French cultural identity from both optimistic and pessimistic perspectives in the face of a rapidly changing world.

Dr John Girling has been a Senior Research Fellow at the Australian National University. He is the author of the acclaimed *America and the Third World* and *Thailand: Society and Politics*. He is also the author of *Corruption, Capitalism and Democracy*, published by Routledge in 1997. Dr Girling now lives in Toulouse.

France

Political and social change

John Girling

London and New York

First published 1998
by Routledge
11 New Fetter Lane, London EC4P 4EE

Simultaneously published in the USA and Canada
by Routledge
29 West 35th Street, New York, NY 10001

Typeset in Baskerville by Routledge
Printed and bound in Great Britain by
Creative Print and Design (Wales). Ebbw Vale

British Library Cataloguing in Publication Data
A catalogue record for this book is available from the British Library

Library of Congress Cataloguing in Publication Data
Girling, J. L. S.
    France: political and social change / John Girling.
        p.   cm.
    Includes bibliographical references and index.
    1. France – Politics and government – 1958– 2. Social history. 3.
    France – Foreign relations – 1945– 4. European Union – France.
    5. World politics – 1945 – Economic aspects. 6. National characteristics,
    French – Political aspects. I. Title.
DC417.G565   1998
944.083–dc21   98–18166
                                            CIP

ISBN 0–415–18324–3 (hbk)
ISBN 0–415–18325–1 (pbk)

Contents

Acknowledgements

To Nina, for being herself; to Peter and Angela, for persuading us to live in France; to Patrick Proctor, Mark Kavanagh and Victoria Smith of Routledge, for encouraging me in this project; to Anne Stevens for scrutinizing the text, and for her judicious comments and helpful advice; finally, to *Le Monde*, for being indispensable!

Introduction

Charles de Gaulle, in his memoirs, famously recorded 'a certain idea of
France'. This was 'inspired by sentiment as well as reason', both of which
led to greatness: that is, France's 'exceptional destiny'. Undeniably, the
general left his imprint on postwar France and especially on the Fifth
Republic, shaped in his own image.

My own study is a critical tribute to de Gaulle, expressed in the quotations (from *Le Salut*) at the head of each chapter. But it asks: to what extent
have the ideas and practices associated with de Gaulle survived thirty years
later? What transformations have occurred? What are the prospects for
France at the turn of the century?

France's 'exceptional destiny' is a distinctive way of thinking – and
acting – in regard to the economy, the nation, the state, politics and society.
Gaullist 'specificity' is associated precisely with 'a certain idea' of
economic growth, directed by the state and empowered by the public
sector. It is thus associated with an exalted notion of the state, centralized
and efficient, designed to 'build national power' and to serve the 'general
interest' – as opposed, in de Gaulle's view, to the self-serving 'particular
interests' of the politicians. Moreover, the direction of both economy and
state is entrusted to an exclusively formed technocratic elite, providing
administrative, political and economic leadership, inspired by 'Republican
values', and guaranteeing the welfare of its citizens.

Gaullism, in relation to other countries, is founded on the idea of
national sovereignty combined with cultural universality (France's 'civilizing mission') and thus the projection abroad of power and prestige:
rejecting the 'hegemony' of the superpowers, insisting on equal participation in world affairs and defiantly proclaiming its nuclear-armed
independence.

Thirty years on, all these founding ideas and practices are called into
question. Economic growth remains fundamental, but it is not state-led;
nationalization has given way to privatization (even under the Socialists);

market forces, global competition, economic rationalization and European construction – these are the new determinants.

Abandonment of economic *dirigisme* in itself involves the reduction of state power, as does the policy (from the mid-1980s) of administrative and political decentralization. The abuse of 'exalted' power, whether in the form of corruption, intolerance of criticism or lack of transparency, now faces the opposition of a previously compliant judiciary, and even the prospects of reform (return to the 'law-based state') by the politicians.

Similarly, the technocratic elites are blamed for conspicuous economic failures (usually the result of economic-political connivance), for their arrogant and aloof attitude, and above all for their inability to solve the everyday problems (notably unemployment, welfare costs and 'insecurity') of ordinary citizens. 'Republican values', supposedly inspiring politicians and the elites, are no longer seen as a spur to probity or to effective action, but rather as a ritual incantation in an attempt to achieve instant 'legitimacy'. Even the foreign policy of 'grandeur', the last stronghold of unreconstructed Gaullism, has been cut down to size by lack of resources, by the constraints of European co-operation and – symbolically, to say no more – by the fiasco of Chirac's nuclear-testing bravado.

Thus, the distinctively 'French' style of thought and action, exaggerated in Gaullist rhetoric, is giving way, under the impulse of realism, to convergence with European and international, especially economic, norms. The large consensus shown in this respect by the political parties of Left and Right (excluding the ultra-Right National Front) is reflected in the blurring of former ideological antagonisms amid the recognition that the role of politics is to accommodate to economics.

Conversely, with the diminution of politics (and the eclipse of the intellectuals!), newer elements of civil society have come to the fore: the younger generation (setting cultural standards of a sort), women (more prominent in business, politics and the professions), environmentalists (thinking the unthinkable: actually reducing traffic, because of pollution, in Paris), investigative reporting in certain of the media, and creative work in the cinema, theatre and elsewhere.

All these different strands, constructing definitions of 'belonging' by gender, generation, workplace, family, neighbourhood, leisure, religion or politics, create for each individual both a social and a national identity, neither of which is fixed (as in Gaullist or other stereotypes) since they vary according to time and place.

Such are the ideas and practices – from 'specificity' to convergence, politics to economics, elites to the people, solidarity to individualism and from reason to emotion (de Gaulle's 'sentiment') – that I present in this work. In addition, I have tried to throw more light on French practices by drawing comparisons with 'Anglo-Saxon' countries.

Evidently, I owe much to the books cited within, for I have come only recently – within the past ten years – to aspects of European studies and for a still shorter period to the study of France, certainly an enthralling subject. Mine is a contemporary work, and I have relied a great deal on the excellent reports, summaries of sociological surveys and wide-ranging debates in *Le Monde*. It is only proper to express my appreciation. But, like a mosaic artist, while I make use of pieces produced by others, they fit into a pattern of my own.

Part I

Formative factors

World economy

Historical investigation over a lengthy period of time reveals dominant patterns of activity. These include the spread of capitalism – the single most important factor in shaping the modern world – as well as the establishment of representative institutions (in one form or another) and the provision of mass education: preparing citizens to take their place in industrializing and increasingly urbanized societies.

Such an investigation, in the second place, indicates 'constants' – of which the expansion of capitalism, from its original location in the 'Protestant' West to worldwide acceptance today, is the most striking – and also 'ruptures', notably the volatile, spasmodic development of representative institutions, and discordant strands in mass culture, varying from hedonistic consumerism to strident nationalism.

The common features of capitalism, throughout the world, include private ownership of productive resources, profit motivation, entrepreneurship, large-scale organization and competitive market mechanism. But capitalism as a social phenomenon (as distinct from an economic abstraction) cannot be understood apart from the particular context in which it operates. It is the national, political and social setting, in which capitalism is 'embedded' in individual countries, that provides its specific form: the latter varies from 'laissez-faire' capitalism at one extreme, as in the United States, to 'state-directed' capitalism at the other, as in Japan and to a certain extent in France.

Nevertheless, it is towards the United States, as the largest single economy (still in its dynamic phase) and as the sole superpower, that other economies, in an ever more 'globalized' age, increasingly converge. It is the United States that sets international standards of economic growth, technological invention, transnational enterprise, competition and productivity on the one hand, and the socio-economic policies of reduced intervention by the state, of welfare cuts and marginalized trade unions – in the name of self-reliance and the 'work ethic' – on the other.

Significantly Britain – America's 'Anglo-Saxon' partner – has taken its own abrupt 'U-turn' as a result of the Thatcherite revolution, away from the nationalized industries, state subsidies and controls and the elaborate welfare services of much of the postwar era, towards the American model. But it is also significant that even Japan, under the stress of economic recession, is moving away from its protected domestic market, its life-long employment policy and emphasis on seniority, towards a more open and competitive system. France, too, whether under the Left (the presidency of Mitterrand) or the Right (the neo-Gaullist era) has opted for 'rational' welfare reforms, privatization of an array of nationalized industries, acceptance of European policy constraints, and the need for international competitivity.

1 Economy

Vers l'association du capital, du travail et de la technique, où je vois la structure humaine de l'économie de demain.

(The quotations at the head of each chapter are taken from Charles de Gaulle, *Mémoires de guerre – Le Salut*, Plon, 1959)

France is an important country. Its economy is the fourth largest in the world, after the United States, Japan and Germany. It is also the fourth largest exporter; the second (next to Germany) per head of population.

France is internationally recognized for the quality of its engineering and scientific research, invention and production. (There have been several Nobel prize-winners in science in the postwar years, the most recent in 1997.) The country has specialized in advanced methods of transportation (the very fast train, or TGV), airspace industry (Airbus and the Ariane rocket), petroleum prospecting and production, telecommunications, electrical equipment and information technology, including the very successful Minitel, introduced some fifteen years ago by France Télécom, but now superseded by the Internet. France is no less well known for its innovative car designs and manufacture; nevertheless, Renault and Peugeot-Citroën have lost nearly half their share of the world market in the last twenty-five years.

France is a major exporter of agricultural products (second only to the United States). It is celebrated for its fine wines, liqueurs, cheese and other foodstuffs; its perfumes, accessories and fashions are famous the world over. France is visited by more tourists than any other country: tourism itself is a major industry, along with hotels, restaurants and associated services.

The service sector makes by far the largest contribution to the national product: some 66 per cent. Industry accounts for 25 per cent, building and construction about 5 per cent and agriculture only 3 per cent. France is the second world exporter of services, after the United States, especially in finance and insurance.

As Jacques Méraud, a member of the Council of the Bank of France and also an experienced statistician, points out, the ascendancy of the service sector has profoundly changed the French economy and accordingly has radically changed the way in which economic growth is analysed. Whatever the phase of the economic cycle, the service sector is doing better than industry (interviewed in *Le Monde*, 2 September 1997).

This structural transformation has major implications, not only for economic growth, but also for employment – for loss of jobs is a major problem – as well as for France's competitive position in the world economy. Indeed, the French economy is backward, in important respects, in comparison with its competitors (notably the United States, but also Britain and the Netherlands), according to the vice-president of the employers' national council (CNPF), Denis Kessler. France's growth rate is less than theirs, it invests less and it has missed out on new forms of communications technology. Kessler blames compulsory government levies on industry, the extent of the public deficit and the burden of official regulations for 'penalizing' the economy (reported by Alain Faujas, *Le Monde*, 10 July 1997).

Both the past achievements and the present predicament of capitalism *à la française* are revealed by the problems of Renault. The innovative car manufacturer, nationalized after the last war, was one of the success stories of French industry during *'les Trente Glorieuses'* (the 'thirty glorious years' of economic growth, from the end of the war to the mid-1970s). In 1996, however, the firm experienced heavy losses. A year later, it abruptly announced the closure of its Belgian subsidiary. Renault's harsh decision, throwing more than three thousand employees out of work, illustrates the problem of transition from the French tradition of protectionism and state controls (see Chapter 2, 'State') towards the 'Anglo-Saxon' norms of privatization and market forces.

Renault's 'example' has major implications for France's economy, politics and society. Thus:

1   The 'brutal' decision by Renault's director-general to close the factory in Belgium, without prior consultation, reinforces the stereotype of 'capitalism without faith or law', treating workers as if they were commodities. Indeed, the typical Président-Directeur Général (PDG) in France, combining the positions of chairman and managing director, is still reputed for powerful, paternalistic – even authoritarian – attitudes, often resulting in antagonistic relations with employees.

2   A trade union representative admitted, however, that the unions were not strong enough to challenge the decision. This is because the fragmentation and political divisions in the union movement,

especially in France, form a major obstacle to effective 'counter-vailing' power.

3   On the other hand, Renault's plunge into the red called for drastic measures of 'rationalization' to cut production costs and expand its market share.

4   The then Rightist government's protectionist attitude – offering a substantial premium to buyers of French cars – only prolonged the agony. When the government would no longer extend its subsidy for another year, because of the need (in line with the Maastricht criteria for a single currency) to reduce public expenditure, French consumers postponed buying. In addition, the government refused the plan by Renault and Peugeot for the (subsidized) early retirement of 40,000 employees at the age of 55, which had been an integral part of the firm's restructuring process. (Whereas Volkswagen, Renault's rival, was able to save some 30,000 jobs by agreeing with the unions to reduce the hours of work in return for lower wages, Renault's boss said such a solution was 'inconceivable in France'.)

5   The economic context for car manufacturers in Europe was unfavourable: indeed, the market was saturated. Production capacity throughout Europe in 1996 was of the order of 18 million vehicles, while actual sales were less than 13 million. Moreover, unlike Volkswagen, which exported more than 40 per cent of its vehicles outside the European market (and Fiat one-third), Renault and Peugeot managed to export only 15 per cent.

6   The financial need to relocate car plants outside France and Belgium was also a factor. Labour costs in Belgium are already 30 per cent higher than in France and 70 per cent more than in Spain, where Renault now has three plants (as well as two in Portugal, where labour costs are even cheaper).

7   The social implications: Renault's closure of its plant in Belgium, throwing three thousand out of work, with the perspective of further dismissals in France, reflects the wider problem of 'downsizing' throughout the 'developed' world in face of intensified competition. Modern industry and services no longer need substantial numbers of unskilled or semi-skilled workers. The 'information revolution' and automated machinery even do away with skilled workers, foremen and executives. The subsequent spread of part-time and short-term work – instead of a 'steady' job – creates a precarious outlook for employees.

8   The 'semi-privatization' of Renault in 1996 – the government still has a 46 per cent stake – indicates the continuing tension between German-style 'social market' capitalism (reducing protection and abandoning nationalization but maintaining satisfactory welfare

provisions), which is endorsed by governments of Left and Right in France, and Anglo-Saxon laissez-faire separation of economics and politics, implying minimum state intervention in the economy and society.

9   A direct result of policy mistakes in France is that the elites, which have long dominated the state and government, are being subjected to unprecedented popular criticism. Renault's boss, Louis Schweitzer, for example, had followed a typical elitist career pattern. Before taking over at Renault he had been head of the advisory staff (*chef de cabinet*) of the Socialist prime minister, Laurent Fabius, in the 1980s. It was assumed that his political clout with the Socialist government would bring material advantages to his enterprise. In the event Renault's situation worsened, after the collapse of the Socialists in 1993. (Renault recovered by innovation and cost-cutting, in 1997.)

As for the French public, increasingly sceptical about the elites, too many damaging failures and too much corruption could be attributed to the '*énarchie*', that is, rule by graduates of the Ecole nationale d'administration. The ENA, in particular, is the training ground for high officials, chiefs of nationalized (and even privatized) enterprise, and leading politicians, such as President Chirac and Alain Juppé on the Right, and Jospin and many of his ministerial colleagues on the Left. (See Chapter 3, 'Education', and Chapter 6, 'Elites'.)

Indeed, the role of elites, the 'paternalistic' state and protectionist economic management are all, increasingly, being called into account. This is in accordance with France's transition to a more competitive, American-style economy, unencumbered by high rates of public expenditure and costly welfare obligations.

Les Trente Glorieuses

Paradoxically, however, the boom years of economic growth in France, especially in the 1950s and 1960s, did not follow the 'neo-liberal' economic pattern. On the contrary, they were characterized by elitist planning, substantial state intervention and 'directed' industrial enterprise. It was during these years – *les Trente Glorieuses* – that French production soared, more than doubling the standard of living of ordinary people and transforming France's occupational structure. Thus, the rural population (formerly so important politically and economically) was reduced almost to insignificance, the working class was fragmented and 'bourgeoisified' (as participants in the new consumer society), the middle class greatly expanded (to become the largest single formation) and the role of the *classe dirigeante* – the economic, political and social elite – was reinforced.

Two valuable studies of *La France de l'expansion*, by Serge Berstein (1958 to 1969) and by Berstein and Jean-Pierre Rioux (1969 to 1974), bring out the significance of France's economic development during this period, as well as its political and social implications. The decade of the 1960s in particular – the Gaullist years – saw the most spectacular growth rate, averaging 5.8 per cent a year, the highest in Europe and only surpassed among the industrialized countries by Japan. (It was twice the British rate, 2.9 per cent, and considerably more than the American, 3.9 per cent.) Moreover, it followed the substantial rate of growth of the previous decade – 4.5 per cent a year – and was to be prolonged almost to the mid-1970s.

Economic growth was favoured, notably, by the reduction of inflation and by the assurance (after so much political turbulence) of Gaullist political stability. The state played a major role in directing, initiating and regulating the process of development: public expenditure, monetary policy, selective use of credit, mobilization of savings through scmi-official organizations, and the impetus provided by nationalized industries (there were nearly two hundred state enterprises in 1958 that made up more than 13 per cent of national production); all these played their part.

At the same time the French economy was open to competitive pressures from the outside world and it benefited, during the 1960s, from the abolition of duties in the European Common Market. By this time half of French exports went to Common Market countries, compared to only 10 per cent in the previous decade.

French industry was both modernized and concentrated. Three major groups controlled the production of cement, three controlled the internationally important chemical industry and four groups dominated the automobile industry. Household consumption, benefiting from economic growth, increased at an average yearly rate of 4.5 per cent from 1959 to 1973 and there were substantial advances in the provision of health, housing, transportation and leisure.

The social structure of France was radically transformed. Agriculture, the very foundation of traditional France, was modernized. (French farmers benefited considerably from the European Common Agricultural Policy.) Over thirty years, production nearly doubled, while the farm population was reduced by half – to three million. Nevertheless, French industry and services increased even more; by 1974, agriculture represented only 5 per cent of gross domestic product, compared to 17 per cent in 1946. Moreover, many farmers ran up debts in the struggle to modernize; massive protest demonstrations took place in an attempt to bring pressure to bear on their government. Other farmers, losing out, simply deserted the countryside.

Urbanization was the reverse side of rural 'desertification'. By the

1970s, nearly three-quarters of the French population lived in the larger towns and cities, especially in Paris but also in such large agglomerations as Lille–Roubaix–Tourcoing, Nancy–Metz, Strasbourg, Lyons, Marseilles, Toulouse, Bordeaux, Nantes and Saint-Nazaire. Deprived regions also emerged, particularly the sites of the traditional heavy industry (coal, steel, textiles), which suffered from international competition.

The working class was profoundly affected by economic change. Skilled workers, modelling themselves on technicians, expanded to some 3 million. The semi-skilled, uncertain of their future and subject to the often arbitrary authority of foremen and bosses, amounted to more than 4 million. Labourers and the semi-skilled, however, still made up 80 per cent of the work force; among them, youth and women were the most precariously employed (nearly a quarter of the work force in 1974 was composed of women). Migrants, too, especially from North Africa, were strongly represented in building, metallurgy and car-assembly plants. Although the purchasing power of workers as a whole increased annually by 4.5 per cent during the fourteen years to 1973, that of women and the unskilled was less than one-third of the average.

The middle class, not surprisingly, was a major beneficiary of economic growth. White-collar workers increased to well over 4 million (more than one-fifth of the population at work). Even more rapid was the increase in mid-level executives and technicians and, especially, managers and members of the 'liberal professions' – from lawyers and accountants to university professors. The middle class(es) expanded to nearly 9 million in 1975 (more than 40 per cent of those at work).

> Better paid, often tertiary-educated, urbanized, with diplomas, including more and more women, in professions oriented to the future, consuming more, more concerned with their freedom and with cultural development, they imparted a rhythm and aptitude for social mobility to the whole of industrial society.
>
> (Berstein and Rioux, 157)

The middle classes, especially, were strongly motivated to achieve a higher level of professional training and to insist on university education for their children. As a result, there was a huge expansion of secondary education (in state schools) from less than half a million in 1950 to more than 2 million in 1970. During the same period, university students increased from 137,000 to more than 600,000.

> This scholarly explosion . . . took school governors by surprise; they were forced to recruit teachers rapidly, who were mostly trained 'on

the job' and worked often in improvised buildings. At the same time the inadequacy of traditional structures of secondary and higher education, intended to form a small elite, faced the influx of far greater numbers, which could neither be educated under suitable conditions nor trained to meet the new needs of society.

(Berstein, 184; and see also Chapter 3, 'Education')

Finally, as a result of prolonged economic growth, the *classe dirigeante* was also strengthened in its 'leadership' role. Under this label, Berstein includes directors of large financial, commercial and industrial enterprises, as well as members of liberal professions closely connected with business, such as commercial lawyers and technocrats. Also included are high administrative officials, holders of political power, a section of intellectuals and members of the traditional large land-owning class.

Restructuring of enterprise is also among the striking changes brought about by the long economic boom. It has resulted in the replacement of many of the family bosses, including the 'great bourgeois dynasties' of Boussac, Wendel or Schneider, by professional managers and technocrats. Nevertheless, of some 60,000 industrial firms in 1975, not more than 1,000 could be classified as modern enterprises. The heterogeneity of French employers is reflected in the incoherence of the bosses' organiza-tion, the Centre national du patronat français. The CNPF, as Berstein points out, was unable to arbitrate effectively between the interests of the rich, large and powerful concerns, which look to the future, and the mass of small and medium enterprises, attuned to the past. The latter are instinctively protectionist and expect the CNPF to put pressure on the state for more material support, but they are too feeble individually to have much leverage.

At the elite level, contrary to the practice of the Third and Fourth Republics, the Gaullist Republic actively encouraged the fusion of political and administrative power in a highly centralized state. Thus, by the end of the 1960s, nearly one-third of government ministers originated from the higher civil service (compared to an average of 12 per cent in the Fourth Republic). In the sphere of government, as in that of economics, profes-sional competence (shown by possession of a diploma at a superior level) marked the surest means to attain membership of the *classe dirigeante*.

More than half the government ministers during the Gaullist period had successfully passed the competitive entrance examinations for the pres-tigious *'grandes écoles'*, such as the Polytechnique (for engineers), the Ecole normale supérieure (for teachers and academics) and the Ecole normale d'administration (for administrators). More than half the government ministers, after retiring from active politics, then went on to join the boards of directors of public or private enterprises. The number of high officials who acquired leading roles in the private sector (an activity known as *pantouflage*) also increased proportionately – to 28 per cent of those leaving the public service in 1974. Significantly, their transfer to private enterprise occurred especially in those sectors that required a high level of economic and technical expertise, such as banking, the chemical industry, metallurgy and electrical manufacture (Berstein, 204–5).

Global economy: domestic uncertainty

Since the end of *les Trente Glorieuses*, economic conditions have changed radically, creating new problems that require different solutions. What are these circumstances, reflected in social turbulence and political uncertainty, marking such a contrast with the overall political stability and economic optimism of the Gaullist years?

In the early 1970s, President Nixon's 'shock' decision to suspend the convertibility of the US dollar, accompanied by the quadrupling of imported oil prices, indicated the disturbing start of a new era. In France, the Centrist government's response under President Giscard d'Estaing was a swing towards 'neo-liberal' policies of budget austerity, priority to the struggle against inflation, reduction of welfare expenditure, deregulation of financial controls and rejection of the 'over-powerful' state.

When the Socialists gained power in 1981 under President Mitterrand, the pendulum swung back to a neo-Keynesian policy of stimulating economic growth – during a period of stagnation – by encouraging domestic demand (increase in the minimum wage, reduction of hours of work, early retirement with a pension at 60). State intervention in the economy was reinforced by the massive extension of nationalized industries, accounting for about one-third of industrial output, and by state control of some 90 per cent of bank deposits.

The subsequent economic crisis of high budget deficits and heavily adverse balance of trade (imports had risen alarmingly at the expense of French production), accompanied by a surge of inflation and unemployment, marked the end of an 'alternative' policy by the Left. But even the return to neo-liberalism did not end France's economic stagnation: industrial output from 1980 to 1986 averaged only 2 per cent a year in comparison with 7 per cent for West Germany and 12 per cent for Britain during the Thatcher years (Bernadette Galloux-Fournier, *L'Histoire de l'Europe au XXe. siècle*, 38–63).

Meanwhile the 'global' economic environment of the 1990s has even more sharply reduced the margin of manoeuvrability of national governments. In France the impact of international competition has increasingly called into question capitalism *à la française*: that is, the protectionist tendencies of much of French industry, the efficacy of state intervention and, with it, the role of the economic-political elites.

'Globalization', according to the declaration of the International Monetary Fund (Washington, April 1997), is not a zero-sum game in which certain economies succeed at the expense of the standard of living and employment of other countries – a criticism often heard in France. Contrary to the widespread belief in the richer countries that the competitive pressures of the world economy have resulted in lower salaries and 'delocalization' of industries, the IMF argues that all countries benefit from the process. The evident 'disindustrialization' of the West – leaving a 'rust-belt' of uncompetitive 'traditional' industries – is the result of technological progress, not of globalization. Rather than putting a break on globalization, therefore, it is better for Western countries to provide social assistance (where necessary) and professional retraining.

Indeed, in the deregulated world economy (especially in financial markets), according to the economist Thomas Coutrot, governments and firms no longer have a choice: they must gain the confidence of the markets. The latter operate, logically, in accordance with exclusively financial criteria: they arbitrate between short-term profitability and the prospect of devalued industrial stocks. Government fiscal and monetary arrangements, investment planning, wage scales and employee management are no longer decisive instruments of policy. Instead, they are subordinate to the financial arbitration of the market: that is, the judgement whether governments and firms have or have not the capacity to provide a satisfactory return on capital investments according to international norms (*Le Monde*, 10 May 1997). National *specificity*, in other words, yields to international *convergence*. Put in a more homely fashion by P.-A. Delhommair (*Le Monde*, 22 April 1997): where the logic of market power operates, one word from the US Secretary of the Treasury is worth more than an entire speech by the French Minister of the Economy.

The inefficacy of state intervention (through nationalized enterprises, subsidies, regulated markets) is the logical counterpart of the dominance of international markets. Fully representing this strain of economic orthodoxy, the secretariat of the Organization for Economic Co-operation and Development (OECD) in February 1995 criticized the relative lack of profitability of French enterprises – though it agreed that they had successfully reduced their level of indebtedness during the 1980s.

French profitability from 1993 to 1995, according to the OECD report, was estimated at 8.5 per cent, better than Japan (4.8 per cent), but worse than Germany (10.5 per cent) and especially Britain and America (both around 18 per cent). Such an unsatisfactory performance is attributable largely to the public enterprises as well as those only recently privatized. It is precisely these organizations – 'most characteristic of government enterprise à la française' with their 'hard core' of staff and directors trained at the Polytechnique or the ENA – that show the lowest rate of profitability of the enterprises under review.

Nevertheless, the OECD discerned a satisfactory trend, even in France, towards American principles of economic management. 'It seems', the report concludes, 'that the French model of enterprise management is converging towards a system that favours the shareholder' (rather than the state). The 'hard core', French-style, is being dismantled. Recent studies show that the 'French model is moving towards the Anglo-Saxons'.

Two years on, Raymond Barre, former prime minister (1976–81) under President Giscard, weighed in on what he saw as continuing French economic weaknesses. The French economy, he wrote in *Le Monde* (16 January 1997), still suffers from the excessive weight of the public sector. In 1996, French public sector expenditure accounted for nearly 60 per cent of national production, compared to an average of 40 per cent for the seven most advanced nations. The burden of social security payments, moreover, has become intolerable for the French economy. In addition, the extensive regulatory system in France rigidifies economic and social structures and prevents the proper functioning of the market.

Now the global economy, according to neo-liberal Professor Barre, has come to the rescue by mercilessly exposing French weaknesses. It is not because of economic competition that unemployment is so high in certain industries, according to this argument. Given the use of better technology and recruitment of more qualified workers, such industries can compete effectively. 'Globalization', rather, serves to pinpoint the vulnerability of certain sectors, where investment, research and quality of product are all deficient and where the burden of state controls and fiscal levies is too great.

Jean Arthuis, economics minister in the Juppé government, drew a similar distinction between the beneficial action of shareholders in private enterprise (punishing ill-considered risks) as in the United States and the adverse effect on industries where the state is the shareholder. In the latter case, he argued, there are usually interminable delays, which enable 'debatable procedures' to conceal the seriousness of the situation and to cover up losses. Between 1988 and 1993 (i.e. under Socialist governments), for example, there were many disasters: enormous losses by the Crédit lyonnais, GAN (insurance), Crédit foncier and others. Jean Peyrelevade, appointed to restructure the Crédit lyonnais, for a time the largest bank in Europe, confirmed in March 1997 that it had lost some 100 billion francs under 'the totally crazy management of a great bank by one single person [J.-Y. Haberer, his predecessor] unchecked by any internal or external countervailing function'. Although 'megalomania and mismanagement are the main reasons for the bank's losses', concluded *The Economist* ('Banking's Biggest Disaster', 5 July 1997), 'fraud is also to blame'; the journal estimated fraudulent transactions at some 10 billion francs as auditors uncovered the bank's 'dud loans'.

Yet another lamentable story, symbolizing *'capitalisme à la française'*, according to Babette Stern (*Le Monde*, 13 May 1997), is the collapse of the largest of the nationalized insurance firms, UAP, after a loss of more than 6 billion francs in 1996, and its subsequent take-over by the private firm AXA. During its thirty-year history, UAP had six presidents. The first, a former inspector of finance (a typical elite post), retired. The second was appointed by Finance Minister Giscard, though it was contrary to the recommendation (another inspector of finance) of President Pompidou. The third was a Socialist and former prefect (unusually, a woman). She was considered close to François Mitterrand, who had recently defeated Giscard for the presidency. Unfortunately, she took over when UAP was not doing too well. But neither she nor her successor was able to control the firm's erratic adventures in real estate – nor did they prevent the heavy losses involved in purchasing a bank. This fourth president was replaced by a staunch Gaullist: for the government, 'cohabiting' with President Mitterrand, had changed. He had just time to start buying up the British Sun Life company before dismissal by the incoming Socialists. His replacement was, of course, a Socialist supporter: this was Jean Peyrelevade, a former deputy director of Socialist Prime Minister Mauroy's advisory staff (*cabinet*), and since 1993 head of Crédit lyonnais. Neither he nor any of his predecessors had ever worked in an insurance company before. Peyrelevade just had time to pursue the acquisition of Sun Life – as well as buy up 'blocking shares', at a cost of 14 billion francs, in another concern – before he, too, had to depart when the Socialists were heavily defeated in 1993 at the polls. Then came the final president, another total novice – but a former adviser to Jacques Chirac – who was left with all the losses. By November 1996 there was nothing for him to do but hand over to AXA.

Now, the European Commission at Brussels has sternly criticized the laxity of French governments in allowing state enterprises to run up such enormous losses and for inadequately supervising them in the first place. The Commission calculates (Philippe Lemaître, *Le Monde*, 3 April 1997) that successive French governments, both of the Left and of the Right, have provided 190 billion francs of public money since 1992 to stave off the bankruptcy of certain nationalized entities. Among the notable beneficiaries have been Crédit lyonnais (some 45 billion), Air France (20 billion), GAN (13.8 billion as well as 9 billion in guaranteed funds) and Thomson (13.9 billion in all).

Yet another source of laxity, also receiving belated correction, is the failure to sanction major enterprises which produce misleading statements ('lies' according to the Commission for the Operation of the Stock Exchange). The Commission deliberately spoke out against such malpractices – alienating domestic and especially foreign investors – as part of the strategy of adapting the French economy to the exigencies of Europe and the wider world. In the Commission's report, some of the biggest French enterprises – this time in the private sector – such as the supermarket chain Auchan, the insurance giant AXA and the huge conglomerate La Générale des eaux – were named.

The Stock Exchange Commission then called for the adoption of the norms set out by the International Accounting Standards Committee, arguing that investors required accurate information that reflected confidence in French business. At stake, argued the Commission, was 'the capacity of our country to mobilize, via the financial markets, national savings for the benefit of our enterprises'. Commenting on the Commission's stand (*Le Monde*, 30 April 1997), F. Bostnavaron and A. Leparmentier note that Crédit lyonnais, GAN and Alcatel (the major French telecommunications and electronics firm) had all published misleading statements in the past with impunity. Now, however, it was the pressure of foreign investors that 'made French bosses realize that the Stock Exchange is not a casino where fortunes can be made as a result of insider trading'.

Modernization

Times are changing, reported Eric Leser (*Le Monde*, 24 September 1997), from the period when *capitalisme à la française* reflected the power of the state, the importance of protective networks and the defensive solidarity of boards of directors, who covered up mistakes and resisted the pressure of shareholders. Four large take-over bids, which previously would have created a storm among complacent heads of enterprises, were now met with relative indifference. Two important amalgamations involving recently privatized industries – AXA and UAP, previously mentioned, and Lyonnaise des eaux and Suez – along with the emergence of a new generation of bosses at the head of such major concerns as Suez, Alcatel, Générale des eaux (a massive conglomerate), Société générale and Peugeot, and the disentangling of interlocking networks, all indicate the 'mutation' of French capitalism, although not without resistance, towards the Anglo-Saxon economic model centred on financial markets and the satisfaction of shareholders. (But note the more sceptical approach of Martine Orange, pointing to lack of transparency and continued multiple crossholdings by directors, contrary to the 1995 Vienot Report on professional ethics: *Le Monde*, 7 November 1997.)

To define a realistic strategy, however, as a fund manager told Leser, obliges firms to be well managed, to seek out the most profitable activities and to attain a 'critical mass'. The American bankers JP Morgan had earlier foreseen greater economic concentration in Europe, partly because economic growth by itself was insufficient to assure profitable development, but also because of the speeding-up of deregulation, the rapid concentration in such important sectors as financial services, distribution, chemicals and pharmaceuticals, and market pressures on firms to adopt clear strategies. The anticipated launching of the unified European currency in 1999 is also a strong inducement to form larger enterprises and prepare to meet increased competition.

Moreover, the large French firms are actively pursuing export markets in Europe, the United States and Asia. Their economic performance, too, has improved. Thus, the oil firms, Total and Elf-Aquitaine, as well as Danone, Lagardère, Schneider and Alcatel, have all benefited from intensive reconstruction over the past years – at the cost, often, of suppressing jobs. (See, for example, François Morin, 'Changes at the heart of French finance', listing the eighty-eight largest industrial and financial groups and eighteen biggest banks, followed by an analysis of production: *L'Etat de la France 97–98*, 424–38.)

To conclude, briefly, with the effect of economic change on French society. It is evident that the unfettered growth of the economy, which is more and more in line with market forces, has not only beneficial but also adverse social consequences. Nevertheless, the 'traditional' policy of protectionism, state controls and elaborate welfare provisions has been equally unsuccessful in limiting the surge of unemployment and of precarious forms of work. (For their impact on French society, see Chapter 12, 'Identity'.)

In an ever more global economy there are clearly limits to the 'autonomous' power of national governments to solve social and economic problems. This is reflected in the narrow range of differences between the economic proposals of neo-Gaullists and Socialists during the 1997 legislative election campaign: and yet the economy was the one area of major concern to both sides! (On the state of political-economy in France, see Chapter 7, 'Parties'.) Under these circumstances, is it really feasible, as former president of the National Assembly Philippe Séguin contends, to reassert the 'primacy of politics' in face of the market, which 'seems to be the new master of the game, imposing itself on our societies as a result of globalization'? Nevertheless, he was right to warn, in Brussels on 6 January

1997, that the market economy is 'in process, no more and no less, of imposing itself against democracy'.

References

Berstein, S. (1989) *La France de l'expansion*, vol. 1, Paris: Seuil.
Berstein, S. and Rioux, J.-P. (1995) *La France de l'expansion*, vol. 2, Paris: Seuil.
The Economist, 5 July 1997.
L'Etat de la France 97–98, Paris (1997) La Découverte.
Galloux-Fournier, B. (1995) *L'Histoire de l'Europe au XXe. siècle*, vol. 5, Paris: Complexe.
Gaulle, Ch. de (1959) *Mémoires de guerre – Le Salut*, Paris: Plon.
Le Monde, various.

State, nation, society

The state

There is a world of difference between the marked distrust of the state, characteristic of American opinion, and the exalted view of the state, derived from the absolute monarchy in France, reinforced by Jacobin and Napoleonic Centralism, and revived by de Gaulle in the Fifth Republic.

American attitudes towards the state are canonized in the words of Thomas Jefferson, author of the 1776 American Declaration of Independence:

> We hold these truths to be self-evident: that all men are created equal . . . that to secure these rights ['life, liberty, and the pursuit of happiness'], governments are instituted among men, deriving their just powers from the consent of the governed: that whenever any form of government becomes destructive of these ends, it is the right of the people to alter or abolish it, and to institute new government.

Thus, a head of state 'whose character is . . . marked by every act which may define a tyrant is unfit to be the ruler of a free people'.

For Americans of this period, and later, people are at the heart of society, not the state. 'Our ancestors', to quote Jefferson from an earlier document (1774), 'were the free inhabitants of the British dominions' and possessed the right of 'establishing new societies' under their own laws and regulations. And if an alien, oppressive and unrepresentative state abuses its control, then 'power reverts to the people'. It was Jefferson's friend, James Madison, who then prescribed the 'separation of powers' and 'checks and balances', so characteristic of the American Constitution, in *The Federalist Papers*.

There can hardly be a greater contrast than this people-centred, almost anarchic, view of authority, resulting in the present fragmented state of the separation of powers, and the evocation of 'grandeur' by Louis XIV ('L'Etat c'est moi!'), by Napoleon, and by de Gaulle: 'The [French] nation understood by instinct', he wrote in *Le Salut*, that it would be menaced by anarchy if he were not there as provisional head of government to lead it to grandeur and 'to serve it as guide'.

British history, by contrast, inclines more towards American distrust of the state – and for the same reasons. British parliamentary government itself arose out of the struggle of 'free-born Englishmen' to prevent the Stuarts from establishing an authoritarian, bureaucratic monarchy on continental lines. Leading the resistance to the 'royal prerogative' were the 'common-law' judges opposed to the centralized dictates of Roman law. Parliament (dominated by nobility, gentry and merchants) in turn defended 'the liberties and free customs of this realm'. The later emphasis on voluntary service by the local gentry as justices of the peace and commanders of the militia (along with a tiny standing army) also provided a remarkable contrast with the powerful armies of absolute monarchs engaged in incessant dynastic wars.

The nation

As for the related formation of the 'nation', this too differs in the 'Anglo-Saxon' countries from the situation in France. The kings 'of France' – and not, until Louis-Philippe, 'of the French' – necessarily had a strategic concept of the nation, directed against the hostile or separate 'other': the English, the Burgundians, the Spaniards. With the formation of a strong unified kingdom, 'natural' boundaries – the Alps, the Rhine, the Pyrenees – became in time national ones. France itself became more culturally and emotionally homogeneous when its arbitrary and oppressive 'feudal' element was eliminated by the French Revolution, which in turn fought for its survival against foreign invasion. This was the 'nation in arms'.

American experience, while sharing the struggle for national independence against the 'alien' tyrant, was very different. The heroic period of the formation of the American nation took place in the nine-teenth century: first, through the 'colonization' of the vast hinterland by soldiers and settlers; second, by the definitive unification of the nation – following the defeat of the secessionist, slave-owning South – in the image of the capitalist and puritan North; and finally, with the 'melting-pot' absorption of millions of immigrants, rejecting the miseries and persecutions of Europe for the dream of a better life. Indeed, the 'American dream' – cradle of freedom, land of opportunity – symbol-izes the nation of the New World.

The English – later the British – experience of the nation shares some of the characteristics of the other two. The 'nation' of sturdy, indepen-dent yeoman-farmers and soldiers, fighting victoriously in France for Harry of England, was a myth concocted by the Tudor kings to demon-strate their legitimacy, brilliantly aided and abetted by Shakespeare. But, contrary to the alienated peasantry of France, the English yeomanry did form part of the nation, along with merchants, gentry, nobility and monarchy. And by the eighteenth century it was a much more commercialized country than France. The English aristocracy was famous for its agricultural innovation and enterprise; the puritan middle class (disbarred from state employment) became the driving force of the industrial revolution; and London had long been the financial centre of the world. It was not until the following century, however, that the 'United Kingdom' was undeniably transformed into the 'Two Nations' of Disraeli's depiction: division between the rich and the poor.

Society

The gap between rich and poor, or 'social fracture' in Jacques Chirac's expressive condemnation – employed to good purpose in his presi-dential campaign in 1995, and then conveniently forgotten – is, of course, common to most if not all developed countries. But what is 'exceptional' in France, besides the unusual character of the state, is first of all the extensive power of the elites, who form a closed circle of administrative and political as well as economic leaders, graduated from the *grandes écoles*. Second, there is the theoretical appeal of 'universal' principles, derived from the French Revolution and the formation of the Third Republic, which now have a ritualistic flavour. Finally, there is the desire to project power abroad on a 'grand' scale, worthy of a great nation.

It is important to note that these very distinctive forms of theory and practice have little or no equivalent among France's neighbours: Britain's 'mandarins' are a pale reflection of the French elites, for instance, while British postwar governments were busy relinquishing rather than extending overseas power. But it is equally significant that these 'specificities' are no longer taken for granted in France. Now, under the impulse of major economic, political and social changes, they come under increasing criticism and even contestation, as the following chapters show.

2   State

L'idée de l'Etat . . . une institution de décision, d'action, d'ambition, n'exprimant et ne servant que l'intérêt national.

Charles de Gaulle

In France, the traditional pull of the state is strong, with a tendency to abuse power. A contrary trend is towards a liberal, de-centred state, with reduced economic role. Finally, there is the renewed inspiration of an ethical, law-based state.

What is 'the state'? The state is the ensemble of structured activities permitting the survival and maintenance of economic, political and social life in a given territory. The defence 'staff' assures external security, the police provide 'law and order', the judiciary arbitrates, preserves property and enforces (especially economic) contracts, the educational system forms citizens – socialized to obey appropriate norms and codes of behaviour – and recruits officials to ensure by their probity and efficiency the legitimacy of the state. Professionalization of functions and continuity of administration are the two main characteristics of the modern state.

How the state administers and *what purpose* these functions are designed to ensure: these are the questions that define the role of the particular, concrete state – notably the fragmented 'night watchman' state of minimum functions, as in America, at one extreme, and the 'exalted' nation-state, promoting economic growth and with it the projection of power and assertion of 'grandeur', at the other (Gaullist) extreme.

The exalted state has an obvious affinity with a *dirigiste* economy, just as the night watchman state, with functions limited basically to law and order, relates to the laissez-faire 'separation of powers' and the differentiation of politics and economics. Politically and administratively, the exalted state adheres to the Jacobin conception of centralization and functional efficiency, inaugurated during the French Revolution, just as the night watchman state prefers the (dissident Girondist) notion of liberty and democratic decentralization. In educational terms, the exalted state promotes a meritocratic elite, while the 'democratic' state stands for the education (and instruction) of the masses. As for 'Republican values', both the Jacobin and Girondin interpretations represent the interests of the emerging middle class (rejecting the traditional values lauded by landed aristocracy, professional army and 'obscurantist' clergy).

These antagonisms, in altered form, are still evident today, as are the tensions between individualism and solidarity, which also reflect divergence between elitist and democratic conceptions. Finally, the exalted state, as noted above, corresponds directly with the aspiration to 'grandeur': a dream of greatness (or a founding myth) which nevertheless confronts the reality of a shrunken presence.

Here, as elsewhere, the 'specificity' of de Gaulle's ambition for France gives way, increasingly, to convergence with more realistic, international norms. Thus, the notion of the state – exalted or limited – plays a major role in regard to the 'formative factors' presented in Part I of this study: the economy (where convergence is already apparent, demanding a more restrictive interpretation of the state), the educational system, Republican values, and the external relations of France, Europe and the world.

Now, the continuing tension in France between the exalted and the night watchman conceptions of the state is evident in two recent statements. The first is by the neo-Gaullist President Chirac, asserting that

> in the continuity of the French conception of public service, the state increases its capacity to serve citizens better, to improve its role as guarantor of the general interest, to contribute more to strengthening social cohesion as well as the global competitivity of our country, the two being intimately linked.
>
> (quoted by Rafaële Rivais in *Le Monde*, January 1996, reprinted in *Dossiers et documents*, April 1997)

What more could one say?

The second is by Alain Houlou in 1989 (also reprinted in *Le Monde*'s *Dossiers et documents*, April 1997) noting that the French revolutionary discourse is of national, rather than 'popular', sovereignty. (Popular sovereignty is derived from the 'social contract' theories of the Anglo-Saxon countries.) National sovereignty is, of course, much more in line with French traditions. Houlou, nonetheless, appeals for greater concern for 'the people', particularly because of the trend towards a more technocratic and functional state in France, which he claims marginalizes its citizens. The emphasis, as he points out, should instead be on 'civil society', marking a distinction between private and public spheres; but this is a concept foreign to French traditions, borrowing from German philosophy and, one could add, from eighteenth-century Britain. (See also Chapter 9, 'Civil society'.)

De Gaulle: the state

De Gaulle's idea of the state, however, is more personalized than techno-cratic. It stems from his overwhelming belief in his 'destiny': the providential saviour of his country from humiliation and defeat. 'The nation discerned by instinct,' he writes (*Le Salut*, 21), 'that in the trouble in which it was plunged it would be at the mercy of anarchy, and then of dictatorship, if I were not there to serve it as guide and as a centre for rallying together.'

It is this fervent belief in his identification with France that provides the popular legitimacy (rather than the technocratic efficiency) of the Gaullist notion of the state. The object, as always, is the duty of the state to 'build national power' which, in future, depends on the economy (p. 98). Hence the state's 'direction' of the economy by measures of nationalization and modernization, realized in the Gaullist boom of the 1960s. De Gaulle, as head of state, is the incarnation of the nation: 'It is necessary that the state have a head, that is, a leader, in whom the nation can see, beyond everyday fluctuations, the man who is in charge of the essentials and who is the guarantor of its destiny' (p. 240).

But in this grandiose vision it is nevertheless election by the people (de Gaulle's great constitutional reform of 1962 was approved by referendum) which imparts legitimacy to the head of state. As President de Gaulle proclaimed in his 31 January 1964 press conference:

> We behave in such a way that power . . . emanates directly from the people, which implies that the head of state, elected by the nation, must be the source and holder of power . . . that is what was made clear by the last referendum.

(Berstein, *La France de l'expansion*, 123–4; Vincent Wright, *The Government and Politics of France*, 14)

Above all, the people–de Gaulle relationship represents the 'general interest' (as decided by the general), while the derided political parties represent faction, self-interest and even anarchy. 'It is necessary that the executive, destined to serve only the whole community,' according to de Gaulle's idea, 'should not proceed from parliament, which brings together the delegates of particular interests.' It follows 'that the head of state does not emerge from a party, that he should be designated by the people, that it is for him to nominate ministers, that he possesses the right to consult the country ... and that ultimately he receives the mandate to assure, in perilous circumstances, the integrity and independence of France' (*Le Salut*, 240).

De Gaulle, it may be said, embodies as a result of popular election the Rousseauist vision of the 'general will', which alone serves the common good. The political parties, which are of necessity 'intermediaries' in the political process, must by Rousseauist and Gaullist definition represent only particular, sectional interests.

> To the divisive character of the parties, which aggravates their weakness, is added their decadence . . . .This is because their passion for doctrine, which in the past was the source, the attraction and the greatness of the parties, cannot maintain itself intact in this era of materialism, which is indifferent to ideals. No longer inspired by principles ... they inevitably become degraded and retreat into the defence of purely sectional interests.
>
> (p. 239)

Given this view, the prime minister, supported by a majority among the party members in parliament, and the president, chosen by the nation, cannot be considered on the same level. As Berstein puts it, the president alone is the incarnation of the state and it is only by delegating part of his supreme power to the prime minister that the latter is enabled to share in the management – a conception far removed from the letter of the constitution (Berstein, 123).

Equally problematic, but constitutional, is the power of the president to dissolve the National Assembly one year after elections and call for new elections. This is a threat that hangs over even the most stable government when president and prime minister, as with Chirac and Jospin, 'cohabit' as political opponents. (See Chapter 7, 'Parties'.)

De Gaulle's practice conformed to his exalted view of the powers of the head of state. The prime minister's private office of advisers, or *cabinet*, was entrusted to loyal followers and certain high officials, who often appeared to be the real government of France, where the ministers only ratified their decisions. The president himself created a kind of super-*cabinet* at the Elysée, also consisting of technical advisers and faithful supporters.

> In principle, this super-*cabinet* [i.e. advisory staff] did not interfere in the activities of the ministers concerned. But in reality the power of this group, in contact with the chief centre of decision, is so strong that despite the desire of the head of state not to create a parallel

structure it inevitably takes over from the minister once a problem passes into the 'reserved domain' [of presidential power].

(pp. 88–9)

Has the Fifth Republic, as a result of Gaullist distrust of the political parties, now become an 'administrative state'? Wright does record the growth of state intervention following greater demands for social security and fuller employment and as a result of increasingly technical and costly economic policies.

> More than ever, the state has become an employer of men, an owner of property, a manager and modernizer of the economy . . . a guarantor of its social welfare: its two million agents now constitute more than a tenth of the total work force.
>
> (Wright, 100)

And yet he notes that, despite the Gaullist vision of a modern technocratic state administered by a favoured elite (see Chapters 3, 'Education', and 6, 'Elites'), the ambitious national plans for the economy have often proved to be ineffective. Second, the notion of nationalized enterprises acting as the 'motor' of the French economy failed to survive the crisis of the early 1980s and has been largely replaced by 'privatization', in line with market forces, instead. Third, although politicization of the civil service has become more and more evident – 'it is difficult to know where the civil service starts and the government ends' – yet 'a close look at the French administration raises nagging doubts about its so-called omnipotence' (pp. 112–13).

While high officials have a keen sense of their technical competence and disinterested guardianship of the national interest, and view the politicians as ambitious and self-interested, the latter decry the administration as 'antediluvian, lethargic and generally obstructive . . . where precedent reigns supreme, where habits are sacrosanct [and] where innovation is frowned upon' (p. 116).

Moreover, the administration itself is weakened by 'the existence of rival networks', often organized around or by a powerful personality, as well as by 'deep-seated ideological cleavages' (pp. 119–21). Anne Stevens, a former British civil servant, also asserts the 'lack of cohesion, incoherence and conflicts' within the French administration, which is 'a major limitation upon policy formulation and implementation' (*The Government and Politics of France*, 153–7).

Raison d'Etat

Yet, despite the evidence of administrative 'fragmentation' – largely the result of personal as well as doctrinal disputes: a heady mixture! – the practice of an exalted state, if not effectively checked by parliament or public opinion, can readily lead to abuse. *Raison d'Etat* has frequently been invoked to justify or to conceal power-ploys, which have little to do with 'national interest' – and still less with 'the lawful State', *l'Etat de droit* – but much to do with personal ambition and external aggrandisement.

The sinking of the Greenpeace flagship *Rainbow Warrior* in New Zealand, authorized by Charles Hernu, the Socialist minister of defence – a man later revealed to have been an agent for the Soviet bloc! – is an example of the latter (the abuse of 'grandeur'). The scandal of *'l'affaire des écoutes'* (illegal wiretapping), organized by the secretive staff of President Mitterrand under cover of counter-terrorism activities, is a case of the former (personal and political ambition).

In March 1993, the newspaper *Libération* published recordings of telephone conversations by Edwy Plenel, reporting for *Le Monde*, who had been investigating the Greenpeace affair as well as corruption in high (indeed the highest) places. More than a hundred examples of requests for wiretapping, from 1983 to 1986, were reportedly aimed at other journalists, lawyers and an actress (no doubt, compromising). These requests from the Elysée's counter-terrorism unit invoked 'arms trafficking' and, naturally, the 'security of the president of the Republic'.

Two years later, following the suicide of an officer of the gendarmerie, who had been in charge of the wiretapping operations, Judge Jean-Paul Valat obtained a computer printout of more than 5,000 telephone recordings revealing the names of those running the 'counter-terrorism' unit and of the twenty-three people who had been targeted. The Paris court of appeal then ruled (in September 1996) that the Elysée unit had been engaged in espionage, which not only infringed the 'intimacy of private life' but was also contrary to the Constitution. It was evident from the documents available to the judges that Mitterrand himself was directly involved. A dozen officers, including a former prefect (head of the unit), a general of the gendarmerie, a deputy-director of President Mitterrand's *cabinet* during the 1980s (Gilles Ménage) and the head of the *cabinet* of Socialist Prime Minister Fabius, Louis Schweitzer (who, admittedly, had reservations about the scheme), were inculpated.

Two features of this sordid affair are important. The first is the recourse to *raison d'Etat* – in this case, the so-called *'secret-défense'* – to prevent 'national secrets' being publicly disclosed. Even the neo-Gaullist Prime Minister Juppé invoked this principle in April 1997. He did so, hardly out of concern for Mitterrand's presidency, but for fear of a precedent being established, which he saw as potentially harmful to any government, whether of Left or Right. 'The state', he explained, 'has the responsibility of protecting, by the defence-secret, persons, missions, procedures and structures, in the interest and the security of the national collectivity.' He did, however, commit himself to 'putting an end', not to the system as such, but to particular 'practices which are totally to be condemned'. It was the incoming Socialist prime minister, Lionel Jospin, distancing himself from the excesses of Mitterrand's last seven-year term as president, who refused the protective alibi of the '*secret-défense*'.

Le Monde aptly commented in its editorial (12 April 1997) that the balance in France between the state and the individual is not always equal, and the penal code shows it. To violate the defence-secret is to risk seven years' imprisonment. To violate the private rights of a citizen (by wiretapping) risks seven times less: one year of imprisonment.

> This gap illustrates, in this country, the weight of a state-culture where the rights of the state override too often the freedom of the individual . . . .This is really what is at stake: the defence of individual liberties against abuse of power by the public authorities.

See also discussion of this important principle in Chapter 7, on the current role of political parties.

The second important feature of the affair is the role of the judiciary. It was Judge Valat who revealed the existence – and the abusive practices – of the Elysée's counter-terrorism unit and who inculpated (*mis en examen*) those who had organized the illegal wiretapping. On the other hand, it was the head of the parliamentary majority, Prime Minister Juppé, who tried to prevent disclosure of this 'dirty tricks' operation. Only after the collapse of the Right in the May–June 1997 elections, and Jospin's assumption of power, was the attempt made to restore legitimacy to the political system by shifting the balance in favour of *l'Etat de droit* – the 'lawful state' – and not *raison d'Etat*.

Decentralization

The exalted state has also been weakened – this time to the credit of Mitterrand's presidency – by the important programme of decentralization inaugurated by the Socialists in the 1980s. Contrary to the 'Jacobin' tradition, Gaston Deferre, minister of the interior, embarked upon a process designed to reverse the centralizing policies of the state, based on the capital. (The Paris region, with only 2 per cent of national territory, houses 20 per cent of the nation's population, 35 per cent of business headquarters and 60 per cent of its research scientists.) As a result of decentralization, Wright points out (pp. 294–6), the government increased the political power of local elected officials by transferring executive responsibility to the regions and departments. The administrative and financial powers of the prefects – traditional agents of the central state – were correspondingly diminished.

Second, new powers were granted to the local authorities: the communes had increased authority over planning, especially in towns of over 10,000 inhabitants; and the departments had greater powers in health, social welfare, education, road maintenance and school bus transport. It is the bigger towns and the departments that have gained most from the reforms.

But major problems remain. In particular, there was no attempt to allocate rationally the functions of the various local authorities: existing powers were left intact and new ones just added. Thus, France continues to live with its 36,000 communes, 96 departments and 22 regions – one of the most fragmented systems of local government in Western Europe (Wright, pp. 297, 309).

Further, the Socialist government would not reform the internal decision-making structures of local government: the power of local elites – the *notables* – is still characteristic of French politics. 'The interpenetration of local and national elites, which is one of the most distinctive features of the French system,' in Wright's judgement (p. 322), 'completely distorts the formal relationship between certain *notables* and the state officials'; for the latter are expected to and do provide preferential treatment to 'local political bosses with extensive Paris contacts'.

The reason for failing to follow through with more effective reforms was precisely the need felt by the government, as Jean Charlot points out, to retain the support of the local political bosses in order to carry out the programme of decentralization in the first place! Because of the effective lobbying of local leaders, who were (and are) strongly represented in the National Assembly and the Senate, the result was to frustrate the central government's efforts both to achieve better co-ordination at the local level and more effective supervision of public works contracts – with their obvious potential for corruption (Charlot, *La politique en France*, 220–5; on corruption, see Chapter 8, 'Affairs').

The centralized state continues; but it is more by connivance than, as in the past, by direct assertion of power. Above all, the economic role of the state has been severely reduced and, with it, its patronage of extensive social welfare networks – precisely because of the pressure to reduce public expenditure in accordance with the tenets of economic orthodoxy. (See also Jacques Chevallier, 'Evolution of the Debate on the State', in *L'Etat de la France 97–98*, 543–6, especially the 'crisis of the state' and its adaptation to changed conditions.)

Jospin's apparent reassertion of state authority (19 June 1997) did not in reality greatly alter the situation. His conception of the state was expressed in ringing tones: 'From the base to the summit of the state, from the official to the minister, only one way to exist, to act and to decide must prevail: that of the service of the nation.' This was intended as a political rather than an economic conception. For Jospin invoked the Republican model and its principle of solidarity which, as Eric Le Boucher pointed out (*Le Monde*, 21 June 1997), is imbued with historic national traditions. But, the writer emphasized, Jospin had to consider the economic constraints within which the system operates: 'The state does not have the means to realize his fine ambition.'

Jospin's aim, accordingly, was neither to re-establish the exalted state nor to diminish its authority in line with 'ultra-liberal' prescriptions (the night watchman state). Instead, like Tony Blair in Britain and for the same (economic) reasons, he has skilfully shifted the terms of debate. Jospin's advocacy is for a different *kind* of state: not the neo-Gaullist 'RPR state' nor the Mitterrandist state, with their tendency to abuse of power, but a return to the 'pure' Republican model of the 'lawful state' – a state that emphasizes moral responsibility to its citizens and therefore regains their respect.

This 'responsible' state must also sustain the vital civic mission of education: for Jospin 'the school is the cradle of the Republic' (Chapter 3, 'Education'). Finally, it is the crucial role of the state, in the context of widespread political disillusionment, to 'modernize our democracy' through the inspiration of Republican values (Chapter 4): 'More than ever, now that public life is suffering from individualism and the reign of money, it is indispensable to re-establish the rules of Republican ethics.'

References

Berstein, S. (1989) *La France de l'expansion*, vol. 1, Paris: Seuil.

Charlot, J. (1994) *La politique en France*, Paris: Fallois.

L'Etat de la France 97–98 (1997) Paris: La Découverte.

The Federalist Papers (1961) intro. C. Rossiter, New York: New American Library.

Gaulle, Ch. de (1959) *Mémoires de guerre – Le Salut*, Paris: Plon.

Jefferson, T. (1776) *American Declaration of Independence*.

Madison, J. (1961) *The Federalist Papers*, intro. C. Rossiter, New York: New American Library.

Le Monde, various.

Stevens, A. (1996) *The Government and Politics of France*, London: Macmillan.

Wright, V. (1989) *The Government and Politics of France*, London: Routledge.

3 Education

La France libératrice, éducatrice, et révolutionnaire ... l'Ecole nationale d'administration, institution capitale qui allait rendre rationnels et homogènes le recrutement et la formation des principaux serviteurs de l'Etat ... jusqu'à devenir peu à peu, au point de vue de la formation, de la conception et de l'action administratives, la base de l'Etat nouveau.

Charles de Gaulle

The 'civic mission' of France, '*éducatrice*' of its pupils in Republican virtues and 'forming' an administrative elite: these are indeed the distinctive features of modern French education. To some extent they are complementary, by establishing a division of labour between the needs of the masses and the needs of the elite. But they are also contradictory, in practical terms, because of the competition between elite and mass education for scarce resources. They are no less contradictory in ideological terms (which in France may be just as important) because of the conceptual clash between 'universality' (i.e. open access to education, even at the highest level) and pragmatic efficiency (selection of an elite) as with the *grandes écoles*, such as the Ecole nationale d'administration (ENA), founded by de Gaulle.

Choices – and costs

In this chapter, I consider the socializing function of education: to produce Republican citizens in the 'mass', on the one hand, and 'leadership' cadres, through a highly selective process, on the other. An overall assessment of the educational system, as such, is beyond the scope of this work. For education is an extremely complicated subject, particularly in France, because of the weight of historical and cultural factors, the continuing if less sharply felt division between Catholic and lay (secular) education, and the competing doctrinal and professional pressures for universal access to education versus 'meritocratic' selection. Yet it is important to note, if only briefly, the reported 'crisis' in the French school system as a whole. It is summed up by Roger Fauroux, a former minister and president of the Association pour l'école, writing in *Le Monde*, 1 August 1997. From primary school to university entrance, he concludes, there is a degree of ignorance affecting pupils and students, who are 'disoriented and badly motivated' and therefore ill-prepared to take on the 'role of active citizens in the world of adults'.

It is this problem that underlies the attempt to combine universality and selectivity – to 'democratize' education and to make it more efficient – that is so characteristic of Gaullism: it is seen not so much as a trade-off but rather as a balancing act. For each form of education ('mass' and 'elite') has to compete for its share of the educational budget. This budget, in turn, amounting to some one-fifth of the total state budget, has to compete with other social interests and demands for government expenditure, which itself expands or contracts according to the condition of the domestic (and international) economy.

'Shares' in the overall budget therefore represent a social choice, since some activities, such as defence, are more highly 'valued' than others, such as culture. In the field of education there is also a choice. But the importance attached both to universal access and to the formation of an elite has a cost: the construction of more and better buildings, recruitment of teachers, university assistants and professors, provision of textbooks and research facilities, financial aid to students, and so on. It is estimated (V. le Billon, *L'Expansion*, 28 August–11 September 1997) that the state spends altogether 444,000 francs to educate a school leaver, but more than twice this amount to train a university engineer, and still more to produce an '*énarque*' or graduate from the ENA.

As for the favoured education of the elite, Claude Allègre, a distinguished earth scientist, adviser to Education Minister Jospin in the late 1980s and himself minister of national education in the Jospin government, calculated in 1993 (*L'Age des savoirs*) that the '*grandes écoles*', with only 4 per cent of the students in higher education, appropriate 30 per cent of the higher education budget!

This highly selective 'choice', so contrary to the universalistic norms of French society (see Chapter 4, 'Republican values'), could be justified only by effective performance after graduation. Elitist leadership in administration, politics and the economy was appreciated during the boom years of *les Trentes Glorieuses*. But with the onset of recession, inflation and rising unemployment from the later 1970s and through the 1980s, followed by conditions of low growth and high unemployment in the 1990s, public acceptance turned to disapproval. The targets of popular scepticism and distrust were not only incapable and 'corrupt' politicians (the 'democratic deficit') but especially the elites, who were regarded as responsible for economic distress (the 'social fracture') of ordinary citizens.

At the same time, the burden of providing for mass education during periods of economic stagnation created major problems for the financially limited apparatus of national education. Lacking the funds to cope with increasing student demands – for more adequate buildings, increased library resources, more and better qualified teaching staff, more relevant curricula and thus better job prospects – the educational system is experiencing a state of crisis. The very different prospects of those leaving school or university illustrate the problem. Thus, in 1995, some 700,000 young people finished their education: 267,000 left at a level lower than the *baccalauréat*; 164,000 passed the *baccalauréat*; and 273,000 left with higher education (including university) diplomas. In the same year, of those who had finished their education four years earlier, 7 per cent with university degrees were unemployed (in 1995), compared to 14 per cent who left after their *baccalauréat*, 26 per cent who had only a low-level qualification (the *brevet*) and more than 42 per cent unemployed who left without any school qualification (*Le Monde*, 22 October 1997).

The crisis in higher education relates directly to the substantial proportion of the budget appropriated by the elitist *'grandes écoles'*, leaving insufficient funds to meet the needs of the universities. One potential source of savings could, however, be found by introducing selective examinations instead of open access to the university; for under the current system a large number of insufficiently qualified or poorly motivated students 'dropped out' after one or more years, 'wasting' student grants and teaching resources in the process.

But to impose the practice of selection on university entrants – although it had been adopted for 'professional' institutes of higher education and, of course, for the *grandes écoles* – was to transgress the sacred right of 'universality'! And even if the educational authorities were prepared to bow to expediency, the students (and would-be students) were not. As Antoine Prost points out, in his remarkable *Education, société et politiques*, de Gaulle himself was convinced of the need for selectivity to prevent the university system from being overloaded. Indeed, he planned to introduce the reform in 1968, but it was swept away by the student uprising (see Chapter 9, 'Civil society'). Yet, as Prost explains (pp. 127, 142), selective entry could have been adopted in 1962, when there were fewer than 300,000 students, but not in 1968 when there were more than half a million. Even the cautious attempt by the Right in 1986 to allow universities to choose their students, without questioning the right of those with the *baccalauréat* to higher education, was abandoned in the face of student protests. (See François Furet, 'United France . . . ', in Furet, Julliard and Rosanvallon, *La République du Centre*, 43.)

Hence the dual crisis of the university system: the costly formation of unpopular elites; and the burden of having to provide higher education for all students, resulting in 'wastage' for some and precarious prospects of employment for others. It is in this socio-economic context that I consider, in this chapter, the three main 'formative' – if also contested – aspects of education in France: first, 'Republican' principles; second, formation of the elite; and finally, selection or universality.

Republican education

Lionel Jospin, although a graduate of the ENA, emphasized the 'Republican' character of French education in his important policy speech of 19 June 1997:

> We [public figures and officials] are responsible citizens of the state in the service of the citizens [of France] . . . .In this way the state can be the true expression of the nation. The nation is not only the living reality to which we are all attached, but above all it is the heart of democracy, which brings together the deepest solidarities. It provides the natural framework for the essential reforms that the country needs.

He went on:

> In the nation, to return to the Republic is first to have faith in the school. The school is the cradle of the Republic. Besides its mission to instruct, it should ensure the apprenticeship of civic virtues. From childhood on, it is necessary to create and sustain a deep feeling of attachment to Republican values, comprising in the first rank *laïcité* [secular education], respect for public matters, and adhesion to an active and responsible citizenship, which all together make up our rights and duties . . . [thus] not only civic instruction but also civic morality.

Secularity (education separated from religious teaching) is the 'supreme French Republican value', affirmed President Chirac in an earlier (March 1997) address to the 'younger generation'. The importance of secular education for 'Republicans' derives from the historic association of the Catholic Church with the *ancien régime*, overthrown by the French Revolution, and the subsequent social and political struggles that divided and still, to a certain extent, divide France.

Chirac went on to approve the re-establishment of civic instruction in school programmes by the then minister of education, François Bayrou, in 1994. His replacement, Claude Allègre, also sought in 1997 to 're-establish civic morality' in schools. But its most ardent champion was the Socialist minister, Jean-Pierre Chevènement, who proposed a 'charter' in 1985 to affirm in the minds (of pupils) the 'moral superiority of the Republican spirit'. (Indeed, the official publication for the first year of primary school, *Education civique: l'Ecole du citoyen*, following the desire of the minister, presented the first verse of the Marseillaise, adding the comment: 'to sing the Marseillaise is to take an active and enlightened step towards Liberty'!)

It was Jules Ferry, a century before, who created 'for the first time in French history, a real national network of free, compulsory, primary, secular schools' replacing the dual system of Church and state schools inherited from the time of Napoleon.

> At every level immense emphasis was put on French language and culture, French history and geography, French national traditions and citizenship. The guiding principle was that a positive set of beliefs and moral values had to be impressed upon each new generation.
>
> (David Thomson, *Democracy in France*, 144)

In a circular letter to primary school teachers, Ferry emphasized their role as a 'natural aid to moral and social progress'. Ferry's official programme of moral education for children between the ages of 11 and 13 includes this section on society:

1   The family: duties of parents and children; reciprocal duties of masters and servants; the family spirit.
2   Society: necessity and benefits of society. Justice, the condition of all society. Solidarity and human brotherhood . . . [a sentence on the dangers of alcohol]. Application and development of the idea of justice: respect for human life and liberty; respect for property; respect for the pledged word; respect for the honour and reputation of others. Probity, equity, loyalty, decency.
3   The fatherland: what a man owes to his country. Obedience to law, military service, discipline, devotion, fidelity to the flag . . . .Rights which correspond to these duties: personal freedom, liberty of conscience, freedom of contract and the right to work, right to organize. Guarantee of the security of life and property to all.

> (quoted by Thomson, 145–6)

It is not difficult to see, beyond the universal principles of justice and freedom, the specific values of the bourgeois Republic: obedience to the law, discipline, devotion to the flag, freedom of contract, right to work and, above all, 'security of life and property'. Indeed, to found the lay school is to found the Republic and with it '*la patrie*', confirms J.-M. Mayeur in *Les débuts de la Troisième République*. 'On the benches of the lay school, beyond class divisions and regional differences, is to be forged the sentiment of national unity' (p. 113).

The same over-arching notion of society, intended to displace class (or religious) differences, is evident in today's manual for children, noted above. Seven-year-olds are presented with a 'series of personages', such as 'Teacher, Prefect, Journalist, Businessman, Mayor', inviting them to 'identify' with these social, political and economic functions, 'which they will study and understand all the better' (*Mode d'Emploi des Ouvrages d'Education Civique*). The textbook's instruction, in general, is worthy and practical (watching out for dangerous objects, hygiene, care for the handicapped, helping in the household, etc.). But every so often an important 'social' message is slipped in: 'there are always rules to respect in order to live in society' (17, 27). The text, not surprisingly, does not ask, 'Whose rules?'

At the other end of the spectrum, in preparation for the *baccalauréat*, is the sophisticated *Histoire Term* (terminal classes, collection J. Marseille). The book, illustrated, replete with graphs, diagrams and statistics, provides contemporary comments and analyses of major themes and events throughout the postwar world. The third part of the book focuses on France since 1945, with chapters on 'The Fifth Republic', 'France Today', 'French Society' and 'France in the World'.

Particularly interesting is the chapter in an earlier section on 'Liberal Democracies Today', covering 'The Great Depression (1973–1993)', 'Detente in Question', 'From the End of the Cold War to the New World Order', 'The Third World', etc. Quoting Lincoln's democracy 'of the people, by the people, and for the people', the text points out that liberal democracy is a 'fundamental exigency' that now 'makes progress throughout the world, even if the economic depression [of the early 1990s] makes it more fragile by enlarging the gap between the wealthy and the excluded' (p. 191).

Democracy, in principle, is said to give primacy to the individual; it guarantees freedom and it strives for equality. Parliamentary, presidential and semi-presidential regimes (as in France) are analysed. The last section reverts to '*Le malaise des démocraties libérales*' and poses three pertinent questions: A privilege of the rich? Dictatorship of the market? Disaffection of the citizens? The text is concerned with the growth of lobbies and the market, which 'also perverts democratic ideals'. Freedom of the press is threatened by 'real financial empires' and 'it is more and more difficult to exercise a critical spirit'. As a result of the economic crisis and cuts in welfare provisions, 'political parties have lost a great deal of their credibility'. Finally, disillusionment and even hatred of the 'political class' have developed since the 1980s, affecting democracies whose 'social project' has broken down (p. 198).

What is one to make of this critical (but realistic) depiction of democracy today? Does this type of argument in an official textbook, so contrary to the soothing statements of the politicians, nevertheless work in favour of the established order, as Pierre Bourdieu suggests? In his study (with J.-C. Passeron), *Les Héritiers: les étudiants et la culture*, Bourdieu points out that even though certain students do contest the efficacy of school teaching, 'one forgets that education substantially succeeds in arousing among its pupils the need for the products that the system dispenses' – that is, the propensity to 'consume knowledge' at the same time as to satisfy it. For the teacher has the initiative. It is he who defines programmes, the subject of courses, work and lectures, 'as well as the quantity of fantasy that can be inserted without risk to the scholarly machine' (pp. 63–4).

Or does the critical analysis of democracy in an official textbook indicate, to the contrary, what Bourdieu in a later work has proposed? In *La Noblesse d'Etat: grandes écoles et esprit de corps* he notes that although the underlying purpose of education is to reproduce the existing social structure and its power relations, nevertheless to give legitimacy to the educational system the authorities have to allow some autonomy to teachers and professors. (Merely to parrot the virtues of the establishment, in a direct fashion, would obviously be counter-productive.) There is always a risk, Bourdieu concludes (p. 553), that those who have been given some freedom to express their own (critical) views – so as to demonstrate the 'impartiality' of the educational system – will then take advantage of that freedom.

This is an important qualification of his earlier study, because it suggests that education, although clearly imparting the values of the dominant groups in society, at the same time may provide a space for alternative or dissident opinions. Whether or not these opinions are influential in changing a given society – at the time or later – is, of course, a different matter.

Note especially, in this regard, Antoine Prost's 'The Democratization of Instruction' (pp. 47–60), on the changing aims of education: from producing good citizens, able to think for themselves, yet unconcerned with the social inequality of pupils and students, to democratization associated with solidarity and success in life (either as skilled workers or as well-educated executives), where social origins are more important than scholarly merit, and culminating in education as 'a commodity, or at least an investment'.

Formation of the elite

Pierre Bourdieu's illuminating study, *La Noblesse d'Etat: grandes écoles et esprit de corps*, exemplifies this process. It can be divided into three parts: the transformation from (superior) social origins to educational 'capital'; the relationship between *grandes écoles* and the university; and the evolution of canons of 'legitimacy'.

Transformation

Bourdieu's thesis is that economic capital and social capital produce social space. ('Capital' is what agents 'invest' in their actions and representations in order to construct a 'social reality' and to communicate with others: see also Bourdieu, *Language and Symbolic Power*, 230.) It is the educational institution which plays a determining role in the reproduction of cultural capital and of the social structure. Accordingly, the recruitment and training of an elite are processes of transformation of inherited capital (superior social origins) to educational capital. Education then provides the scholarly 'titles' that legitimize the domination of the elite in economy, politics and the administration (pp. 13, 57, 537).

The laureates (prize-winners) in the competitive examinations for best secondary school pupils in the late 1960s indicate the principle of selection at work: only one-third are girls, one-quarter are from scientific disciplines and more than one-third are from Paris *lycées*. The traditional training of the elite is in the humanities, especially in French and in philosophy. The examination essays of the prize-winners, especially in these two subjects, thus reveal the types of 'intellectual' quality valued by the 'academy'. They also demonstrate, according to Bourdieu, the kind of social background that is required to succeed. Thus, a division exists between those pupils considered to have 'talent' and those who merely 'work'; the former are well off, have good social status and are substantially helped by their families. It is they – the future elite – who display the 'verbal acrobatics, hermetic allusions, disconcerting references and technical supports' that demonstrate their ability and authority (pp. 30, 45).

Those who are talented look down on the pedestrian, laborious pupils of lower social origins, who are considered to be 'poor, narrow, mediocre, clumsy and confused'. Their 'virtues' are correspondingly modest: attentive, serious, methodical, timid – far from the 'noble' attributes of their social superiors. The latter, moreover, are characterized by their sense of loyalty and duty, their manliness, leadership and public spirit (similar to the 'character' inculcated by the British public schools). This is a 'strange cognitive machine', Bourdieu comments, that carries out a 'whole series of

operations of knowledge and evaluation' tending to establish a strict correlation between classification (by social origin) at entry to the *grandes écoles*
and classification (by scholarly result) at exit – without the principles or
criteria of social classification being ever known or recognized officially
(pp. 51–2, 56–7, 61, 102, 142).

The occupational results correspond to this classification: of fifteen
former students of the highly esteemed Ecole normale supérieure who
were of inferior social status, surveyed by Bourdieu, twelve became
teachers in secondary education and three in higher education (but of
'inferior' disciplines). As for nineteen former students of higher social
status, two went on to become diplomats, two were writers, two were in
secondary education and thirteen were in higher education, including four
in the prestigious Collège de France (pp. 68–9).

Bourdieu's emphasis on social origins has been challenged by Ezra
Suleiman, author of *Elites in French Society*, who argues that how the elites
perform after graduation is more important than their social background.
In his largely empirical study of the functions, interests and power of the
elites, but which is also critical of the concentration of power in France,
Suleiman 'moves away' from the notion of education as reflecting the division of labour in society and thus serving to reproduce the existing class
structure. He tends to support Raymond Bourdon's dissenting view, which
notes the great variation in status of people with the same education as
well as the impact of educational qualifications on their occupations
(Suleiman, 32–3, 280).

Nevertheless, two researchers from the statistical institute (Insee),
Dominique Goux and Eric Maurin, confirm the continuing importance of
social inequality on educational performance and subsequent work.
Reported by Béatrice Gurrey in *Le Monde* (29 August 1997), their studies
acknowledge the progress that has been made in the last thirty years. In
the early 1970s, for example, three-quarters of those at work who came
from working-class or white-collar families had only a leaving certificate;
today, one in five has the *baccalauréat* (qualifying for university). But if the
general level of education has risen, they claim that it operates only to
transfer inequalities to a higher level. They conclude that 'the scholarly
hierarchy respects the hierarchy of social origins hardly less than twenty
years ago'. And again: 'The inequalities experienced by young people at
the start of their active working life today reflect the unequal educational
levels of their parents.'

Olivier Galland in *Le Monde des étudiants* (1995) makes the same point.
Forty years ago the children of workers were forty times less likely to go to
university than were children of senior executives; in 1962 they were only
six times less likely. But in spite of greater mobility, social hierarchies are

still reproduced. In the third cycle of the university (i.e., at doctoral level) half the students are children of senior executives or members of liberal professions, and only 10 per cent are children of workers (reported by Luc Cédelle, special issue on the university, *Le Monde de l'Education*, October 1997).

Children of poor families have practically no chance to go to the *grandes écoles*, concludes Roger Fauroux in the article mentioned above.

> At the same time, a subtle network of information and social complicity allows the socially privileged to place their children in the good classes of the good lycées, serving them as a springboard for the good preparatory classes [of the *grandes écoles*] and so on.

Certainly, entry into the latter requires work and merit, but it is made much easier by the social 'process of segregation'. M.-C. Kessler's study of the *grands corps* shows that nearly two-thirds of this elite grouping belonged to the 'upper classes' in 1975; in 1983, three-quarters of students at the Polytechnique originated from the industrial and financial bourgeoisie (*Les grands corps de l'Etat*, 45–6).

Grandes écoles *and universities*

A similar process of segregation operates, according to Bourdieu, between the '*grande porte*' of entry into higher learning and the '*petite porte*'. The former includes the Ecole nationale d'administration (ENA), the Ecole normale supérieure (ENS), the Ecole des hautes études commerciales (HEC), the Polytechnique and the Institut des sciences politiques (Sciences-po). Sixty per cent of their pupils are from the dominant class. The *petite porte*, on the other hand, provides entry to university faculties of literature and science, technology, applied arts, etc. Only 35 per cent of their pupils are from the dominant class. They are more technically educated and 'narrowly' specialized, in contrast to those entering by the *grande porte*, who are often members of the Parisian bourgeoisie with considerable 'cultural capital'. It is the latter, with their 'general ideas', their culture and their capacity for synthesis, who possess the virtues needed for rapid promotion to dominant positions and authoritative functions (pp. 188–209).

While the ENS gives priority to intellectual values, preparing its pupils for senior posts in education, the ENA's 'promise' of high positions of power – in the administration especially, but also in politics and in the public (but also private) sector of the economy – is unrivalled. The HEC concentrates on commerce and management (pp. 240, 265, 279, 297). Although two-thirds of former ENA graduates surveyed in 1987 criticized the training provided by the *grandes écoles* as insufficiently adapted to the modern world (see also my Chapter 6, 'Elites'), there is still a consensus that the schools are indispensable 'for supplying France with the elites that the university does not provide' (J.J. Gurvicz, *L'Expansion*, September 1987).

Implications of legitimacy

The holders of economic and political power, from Bourdieu's analysis, are more and more invested with the appearance of intellectual legitimacy, as denoted by scholarly 'titles'. The demands imposed by intellectual standards as well as the 'imperative of economic realism' increasingly converge on the American model of the 'responsible expert', most often identified with the economist or the technocrat. Such changes in the field of economic power, especially access to dominant posts through scholarly titles, Bourdieu claims, lead to profound changes in elite and technocratic relationships in the struggle for power. The emergence of salaried executives (supplementing or displacing family owners) is an important example (pp. 305, 405–7, 482, 537).

Nevertheless, the 'symbolic capital' of recognition and confidence in scholarly titles, providing legitimacy to the elite, has its own laws of accumulation (emphasizing credit and prestige), which are not those of economic capital (p. 455). Thus, the *grande noblesse d'Etat* arrogates to itself the notion of a 'universal class' (through its possession, by merit, of scholarly titles) in order 'legitimately' to exercise power. But it also has to live up to the norms of universality. On the one hand, the (economic) elite, for example, is convinced that the 'managerial revolution', reforming the process of decisions in the great private enterprises, will benefit its members in terms of property rights. On the other hand, they also are expected to think in social terms, to behave as 'agents of the state' rather than as businessmen, and thus to base their decisions on 'impartiality', 'expertise' and the ethic of public service (pp. 539, 548–9).

Finally, as noted above, power-holders cannot expect 'effective symbolic service' from their agents without granting them a certain autonomy. The legitimacy accorded to their intellectual status requires that they decide by merit rather than obedience to power. It is this autonomy that provides the potential for dissident decisions and alternative policies.

Here, I have discussed the *educational* formation of the elite, following Bourdieu's analysis. The *practice* of the elite – its economic, political and social interaction and its relationship with the 'people' – is more appropriately taken up in Chapter 6 of Part II of my study. This part, 'Politics', brings together the activity of the elites, their association with political parties, their connivance with economic interests – and the countervailing influence of civil society.

Universality or selectivity

The main problem for the French university system is the massive increase in student numbers in the 1980s coupled with the universal right of entry for all who have passed the *baccalauréat*. All this puts an intolerable strain on limited financial resources, on teachers and on the students themselves. The number of university students rose from 800,000 in 1980 to more than 1,250,000 in 1994. (There were 250,000 new entrants to universities in 1995 compared to 36,000 in preparatory classes for the *grandes écoles*.) This expansion, Rob Turner notes, is largely due to the government's desire for a highly trained work force and to the popular demand for higher education, stimulated by France's high level of youth unemployment (Turner, 'Higher education', 99).

An attempt to limit the right of automatic entry was made by the Chirac government, cohabiting with President Mitterrand, in 1984. But the Devaquet bill was abandoned as a result of student demonstrations. A further attempt in 1995 also failed. Since then the principle of universality has become sacrosanct for both Right and Left.

The *grandes écoles*, on the other hand, with about 200,000 students in a total higher education population of over 2,000,000, have selective entrance examinations – as do other specialized faculties, such as medicine and engineering. A further distinction, noted above, is the social function of the ENA, ENS, Polytechnique and other prestigious schools producing graduates for top management posts, while the universities train future members of the liberal professions, teachers and mid-level civil servants. This elitist function of the *grandes écoles*, as Turner emphasizes, is incompatible with the provision of mass higher education (pp. 102–3). As a result of its favoured status, the selective sector takes the best students and a major share of resources from the open-access sector (p. 112).

The university system, incapable of effectively absorbing such large numbers, faces the related problem of unacceptably high drop-out (or repeat) levels of students, especially in the first two years. Pass rates for the two-year cycle (DEUG) are only about 55 per cent, requiring numerous resits. Even then, fewer than two-thirds continue into the second cycle (*maîtrise*) after three years, while 11 per cent take longer and 19 per cent fail altogether. As Claude Allègre has noted, the system has to cope, in effect, with double the number of students it would have if qualifications were achieved in the time intended (Turner, 100).

Although Prime Minister Jospin pledged in his June 1997 policy statement to give priority to education, he did not commit himself to precise targets. A major problem, given the government's commitment to reduce public expenditure (in line with the Maastricht criteria), is of course the huge funds that are needed to finance the open-access system. A colloquium at the Sorbonne in June 1997 claimed that more than 40 billion francs would be needed over five years, along with the creation of 5,000 more posts for teacher-researchers and an equal number of administrative positions. (As for student grants, which Jospin intends to increase, the objective of one-quarter of students receiving grants has not been attained.) Still another much-debated problem, besides the content of university courses, is that of teaching methods adapted to the diversity of new *bacheliers*, who (as noted above) are insufficiently prepared for their entry into higher education (Michel Delberghe, *Le Monde*, 17 June 1997).

The French higher education system, accordingly, raises three fundamental issues. First, the vital importance of economic growth, which can alone ensure a major increase in public spending (Chapter 1). One must remember, however, that government ability to influence the economic system is limited, either as a matter of positive inducements or, which is perhaps more often the case, negatively as a result of ineffective or erroneous fiscal or monetary policies. Second, the very serious problem of unemployment, especially among the youth, which radically affects job prospects for school-leavers and university graduates (see Chapters 7 and 12). Finally, the question of choosing pragmatic selectivity (as in the case of specialized as well as elitist education) or 'principled' universality (open access to all who 'merit' higher education) despite its evident inefficiency in the use of scarce resources and the unnecessarily heavy strain it puts on currently inadequate facilities.

All the recommendations for reform require a large increase in funds. In addition, a UNESCO specialist on higher education, Georges Haddad, writing in *Le Monde de l'Education*, October 1997, while noting the good quality/price ratio of French universities, proposed more effective links between universities and their cultural, social and economic environment and, what was especially needed, more libraries, documentation centres and information equipment – following the Anglo-Saxon example. (Haddad was responsible for UNESCO's international conference on higher education in Paris in autumn 1998.)

Roger Fauroux, author of a report to the Juppé government, insists in the same issue of *Le Monde de l'Education* on the need to overcome the inequalities in French education, particularly between the *grandes écoles* and the universities: to aid the 'priority zones' in depressed areas; to create proper professional and technological channels with access to the highest levels of education; and, above all, to 'deconcentrate' the 'hyper-bureaucratic' administration of education, thus limiting the state apparatus to its essential functions: defining standards of competence, setting out broad policy measures (without getting involved in day-to-day management), and establishing respect for 'Republican values'.

References

Allègre, C. (1993) *L'Age des savoirs*, Paris: Gallimard.

Bourdieu, P. (1989) *La Noblesse d'Etat: grandes écoles et esprit de corps*, Paris: Minuit.

—— (1991) *Language and Symbolic Power*, trans. G. Raymond and M. Adamson, intro. J. Thompson, Cambridge, UK: Polity.

Bourdieu, P. with Passeron, J.-C. (1964) *Les Héritiers: les étudiants et la culture*, Paris: Minuit.

Education civique: l'Ecole du citoyen.

L'Expansion, 28 August–11 September 1997.

Furet, F. (1988) 'La France unie . . . ' in F. Furet, J. Julliard and P. Rosanvallon, *La République du Centre*, Paris: Calmann-Lévy.

Galland, O. (1995) *Le Monde des étudiants*, Paris: PUF.

Histoire Term (1995) coll. J. Marseille, Paris: Nathan.

Kessler, M.-C. (1994) *Les grands corps de l'Etat*, Paris: PUF.

Mayeur, J.-M. (1973) *Les débuts de la Troisième République*, Paris: Seuil.

Le Monde, various.

Le Monde de l'Education, October 1997.

Prost, A. (1997) *Education, société et politiques*, Paris: Seuil.

Suleiman, E. (1978) *Elites in French Society*, Princeton, N.J.: Princeton University Press.

Thomson, D. (1969) *Democracy in France since 1870*, London: Oxford University Press.

Turner, R. (1997) 'Higher education' in S. Perry (ed.) *Aspects of Contemporary France*, London: Routledge.

4 Republican values

Faire en sorte que l'intérêt particulier soit contraint de céder à l'intérêt général; que les grandes ressources de la richesse commune soient exploitées et dirigées à l'avantage de tous; que les coalitions d'intérêts soient abolies, une fois pour toutes; qu'enfin chacun des fils et chacune des filles de la France puissent vivre, travailler, élever leurs enfants dans la sécurité et dans la dignité.

Charles de Gaulle

Universality – the general interest – inspires the two main sources of Republican legitimacy: Montesquieu and Rousseau. Yet, although they share a common concern for morality and the public good they start from very different premises, in effect conservative and radical. This is why both the neo-Gaullist Chirac, on the one hand, and the Socialist Jospin, on the other, can draw their inspiration from the broad spectrum of Republican values. It is no less important, given the absence of ideological alternatives, as Socialism was in the past, that Republican values are all the more needed as a point of reference.

Montesquieu is, of course, the fervent advocate of liberty, which can only be guaranteed by the 'separation of powers' (as perceived in British parliamentary practice) countering the tendency towards despotic government. But in his sociological approach to politics and society he also argues that laws must be adapted to a variety of conditions. Such is the 'pragmatic' relativity, rather than the doctrinal universality, of laws.

Rousseau is no less strongly identified with the 'general will' of popular sovereignty, which always seeks the common good. Conversely, he denounces the baneful effect on society of 'particular interests'. For Rousseau, human beings are naturally good (once harmful social institutions have been removed) and they project the 'purest' expression of will.

The general will is declared to be indivisible and universal, in marked contrast to Montesquieu's insistence on the importance of 'intermediary' associations in society, which to Rousseau, by definition, are self-serving obstacles to the common good. Montesquieu, one might say, is conservative in his understanding of political power. It is because of the danger to liberty resulting from the concentration of power in one entity (whether absolute monarchy or 'general will') so as to achieve 'universal' goals, that the tendency towards absolutism requires to be checked or 'balanced' by the separation of executive, legislative and judicial power.

So persuasive are the views of Montesquieu that he was lauded by James Madison, 'Father of the Constitution' of the United States, as the 'celebrated Montesquieu', the 'oracle who is always consulted and cited on this subject'. Thus Madison, referring to American experience, warns against the 'danger of disturbing the public tranquillity by interesting too strongly the public passions' which, he says, would occur with 'frequent reference of constitutional questions to the decision of the whole society' (read 'the general will').

Madison takes Montesquieu's argument to its logical conclusion by proposing, as the most effective way of preventing oppression and injustice, that 'society itself will be broken into so many parts, interests and classes of citizens, that the rights of citizens, or of the minority, will be in little danger from interested combinations of the majority' (*The Federalist Papers*, nos 47, 51).

Such is the positive argument for the greatest extent of freedom – in a pluralist society – to safeguard the individual against abuse of power by the state or by the majority (Tocqueville's 'tyranny of the majority'). But there is also a negative side. For the obvious effect of such a fragmented state or political majority is to paralyse concerted efforts (the general will) to achieve important social goals.

These contrary concepts of Montesquieu and Rousseau merge in the French Revolution – iconic source, above all, of 'Republican values'. Consider Sudhir Hazareesingh's distinction between the conservative 'forces of order', attached to the rule of law and private property, and the progressive 'forces of movement', demanding political and social change (*Political Traditions in Modern France*, 80–1; also common values, 66–7).

The Jacobin practice of a highly centralized administration operating under universal rules has long been contrasted with the Girondin preference for regionalism and decentralization. But even the celebrated watchword of the French Revolution – liberty, equality, fraternity – contains no less serious contradictions.

Liberty – to think and act as one wishes (without harming others) as a result of freedom from external constraints – is hardly compatible with the pursuit of equality: that is, to impose equal conditions of life, economically, politically and socially, on existing inequalities. However laudable in itself, the creation of an equal society is bound to infringe on the liberty of the 'haves' for the sake of the 'have-nots'. The practical solution, of course, is to restrict the notion to political and legal equality: that is, equal rights of all citizens to elect their representatives, combined with equality, whether rich or poor, under the law. The result, however, is that political equality conceals economic inequality.

A further interpretation of 'equality' refers to 'equality of chances' – the famous *égalité des chances* much favoured by conservatives today. In theory each pupil, for example, has an equal chance to do well at school and an equal chance – not dependent on birth or wealth, but on merit – to gain entrance to the *grandes écoles*. (But, as Bourdieu has convincingly shown, the scales are in fact weighted in favour of those with 'cultural capital' and superior social origins.)

Similarly, as the historian Michel Vovelle points out in his study of the French Revolution (*La Chute de la monarchie*) civil equality was no problem for those experiencing the transition from feudal society to the world of liberal capitalism: 'Men are born and remain free and equal in rights; social distinctions can only be founded on common utility', according to the revolutionary slogan. In practice, however, the Constituent Assembly distinguished between active and passive citizens, based on economic criteria, which excluded one-third to half of the people (and would have excluded Rousseau himself!). In the revolutionary triad, 'liberty, equality, fraternity', the third term came only afterwards. Security and property came first (Vovelle, 170–1).

For the members of the Constituent Assembly, property was one of the most precious forms of liberty, that of the freedom to dispose of one's goods. A major turning point was the decrees of August 1789, freeing land and people from all forms of (feudal) subjection, affirming the bourgeois conception of individual property rights. Then, in March 1791, the Allarde law proposed 'free contract' as the basis of new social relations, by suppressing the corporations as well as privileged manufacturers. All state regulation of production, on the same principle, was abolished. Similarly, freedom of work was proclaimed to be in harmony with freedom of enterprise. The celebrated Le Chapelier law proscribed, in the name of freedom, any association or combination, whether of guilds or masters, and it forbade them to take any decision based on claimed common interests (pp. 173–4).

Marc Bouloiseau, in turn, has shown how the Jacobins were motivated by a composite ideology, at once spiritual and concrete, individual and social, drawing on Rousseau's writings but simplifying and materializing them. Theirs was an ideology of confidence in the future and they displayed an earnest desire for moral renovation. For Robespierre, in particular, human dignity was inseparable from liberty: it was despotism that corrupted human behaviour. Rights and duties were conjoined in the compact made by citizens with the Republic. Thus, patriotism was not simply an exclusive love for a part of the earth, but comprised the whole nation where the laws expressed the general will. Fatherland, liberty and virtue were inseparable. 'Where virtue will prosper under the laws, where equality will reign among men . . . where man will be as nature made him, free and just, there will be the fatherland of a Frenchman.' Finally, national solidarity guaranteed universal fraternity; and it was France that would lead the way (Bouloiseau, 39–40).

In contrast to the radical themes of the Jacobins, the rival Girondins were more pragmatic and more conservative. Their aim was to establish a Republic of notables with a strong government and a liberal economy. They believed in landed wealth and commercial capital as the twin foundations of social order. In their staunch defence of private property they would not allow confiscation to take place except for declared enemies of the nation (Bouloiseau, 60–1).

The second historic source of Republican values was the formation of the Third Republic following the catastrophic defeat of Napoleon III by the Prussian army and the uprising of the Paris Commune. The conservative leaders of the Third Republic stood for a bourgeois, provincial France. The 'Republican virtues' of individual freedom, equality under the law, tolerance and civic consciousness reflected the rise of civilian politicians (supplanting the aristocracy and the military), of lay professionals (repudiating the influence of the Church) and, more broadly, of a financial, industrial and commercial bourgeoisie and the emerging middle class, partly collaborating with and partly opposed to provincial small-town society and the mass of landholding peasants.

The 'Republican consensus', as distinct from its 'leadership', was more broadly based. Popular support for the Republic was established at three different levels. First, at the socio-economic level, the Republic was seen to represent the interests and the aspirations of the 'small man' – small businesspeople, artisans, shopkeepers, provincial society and the rural majority. Second, at the political level, Republican rhetoric emphasized the dominant role of politics, especially reviving the great themes of the French Revolution: freedom from oppression; independence from an overpowerful and unrepresentative executive; the affirmation of a lay society (liberated from old 'superstitions' and the sectarian controls of the Catholic Church); and the rights of man. Finally, at the political-economic level, the Republican regime ensured its viability by detaching one element of the old order (nobility, Church, wealth) by obtaining the support, or at least the neutrality, of big business and finance, precisely by maintaining the policy and practice of a second, and no less important, set of Republican values: the rights of the individual, reliance on laissez-faire economics and respect for property.

Thus, Montesquieu's advocacy of intermediary groups and separation of powers – compatible with the views of the Girondins – is no less applicable to the practice of the Third and Fourth Republics. The result was contestation by the elected representatives of the powers of the executive, preventing a return to autocracy, but at the cost of political fragmentation and national weakness.

Now, it was precisely the humiliation of defeat in the Second World War (putting an end to the Third Republic) followed by the political and psychological disaster of the Algerian war, revealing the utter incapacity of the leaders of the Fourth Republic, that incited de Gaulle to revive the Rousseauist (and Jacobin) formula instead: a powerful, but popularly elected, executive imposing its legitimate authority on the dispersed and divisive politicians.

Despite the undoubted stability of the Gaullist presidential system, one major problem remains unsolved: how to uphold the political priority of Republican values in a national and international context dominated by the economic. Historically, democratic – and hence political – ideas emerged and were practised in France, America and even in Britain *before* the ascendancy of capitalism. (Democracy in the newly independent United States, for example, effectively represented the ideas and interests of small-scale and relatively equal farmers, merchants and professionals – a situation which is totally unlike that of today.) The context of the French Revolution, too, was basically political: the enemy was the arbitrary and oppressive system of absolute monarchy; the objective was to replace it with the rule of the people.

Gambetta, hero of French resistance to the Prussian army and organizer of the Republican victory consolidating the Third Republic, entirely expressed the primacy of the political. 'For those who believe that the People is the one lawful sovereign, and must really exercise power,' he declared in his 'Belleville Manifesto' (1869), ' . . . then all those who hold any kind of office must be effectively checked, especially the head of the executive power.' Following this bow to Montesquieu, he emphasized: 'I believe that the progress of these social reforms depends absolutely on the political regime and on political reforms: and for me it is axiomatic in these matters that the form involves and determines the substance' (quoted in Thomson, *Democracy in France*, 119–20). Political reforms and civil liberties, in other words, are a precondition of social and economic reforms.

Socially, on the other hand (as noted above), the Republican consensus depended on the economic interests of the peasantry and of the 'new social strata' or middle classes – ranging from small industrialists and traders to members of the free professions (especially lawyers, journalists and teachers), shopkeepers, artisans, builders, salaried employees and petty officials. The alliance of the new strata with elements of the *haute bourgeoisie* symbolized for Gambetta the current success and future direction of the Republic.

Gambetta indeed welcomed in 1877 the 'true leading classes, that is to say, those who think, those who work, those who amass wealth; those who employ themselves judiciously, liberally and in a way that is profitable to the country'. The adhesion of these *classes dirigeantes* to the Republic, conforming to the 'bourgeois traditions of 1789 and 1830', would (he believed) put an end to the antagonism between capital and labour, replacing it with mutual prosperity (Mayeur, *Les débuts de la Troisième République*, 49–52).

It is this amalgam of *political* ideology and *economic* interest that characterizes the 'Republican values' of the French Revolution and the Third Republic – and indeed of today. Only five years after Gambetta's pronouncement, the Freycinet government was to proclaim: 'Nations do not live only by politics; they live also by business and material interests.'

Today, however, those who emphasize the 'values' of the Republic tend to ignore the 'interests' at stake. This is no problem if values and interests are separate or at least interdependent. It is a problem when 'material interests' largely determine the content – if not the form – of government policies, as they do today (see Chapter 7, 'Parties').

There are, however, two things to be said in favour of Republican values, as emphasized by Jospin in his June 1997 policy statement. The first is that support for 'Republican morality', especially at a time when 'public life is suffering from individualism and the rule of money', does set a *standard* by which public behaviour can be judged. If the latter falls too far below that standard then the incongruity between policy (or rhetoric) and practice becomes obvious and politicians are discredited – or voted out of office. (See also the discussion in Chapter 8.)

The second point is that, despite the constraints imposed on policy-making by economic conditions, there is a role for political and social reforms: the emphasis on improvement of health services and education and the programme of constitutional reforms inaugurated by both the Blair government in Britain and that of Jospin in France is an important example. Further, as Jospin puts it: 'The modernization of our democracy does not only presuppose institutional reforms; it demands profound cultural changes.' For French people to become more engaged in public life, according to Jospin, requires an 'evolution of mentalities' and a change in behaviour, in which the Left can lead the way.

To sum up the ambiguity of Republican values: first, they have a mobi-lizing potential (as above); second, they provide instant legitimation (examples to follow); third, they are often little more than empty rhetoric (recall Flaubert's parody in *Madame Bovary*, when Emma encounters her lover amid the platitudes of what would later be taken for a 'Republican' address); finally, in the last resort, they set standards by which public life can be judged.

Clearly, the *ritualistic* invocation of Republican values is intended to provide instant legitimation: it is the French form of 'politically correct'. Here are some examples.

The governor of the Bank of France, Jean-Claude Trichet, is being interviewed by two reporters from *Le Monde* (25 June 1997). The final point they make is about criticism of the composition of the Council on Monetary Policy, which they consider one-sided. (Eight out of the ten members are classed as being on the Right.) Should not this important body reflect the nation's diversity? The governor denies this classification, claiming that the 'most varied experiences' are represented in the Council. Moreover, 'the Bank of France, our money and [international] confidence in the franc are the property of all French people'. To clinch the argument: 'The Bank of France is neither of the Right nor of the Left, it is Republican.'

Consider President Chirac's address at Lille, 7 June 1997:

> Today, my duty [during the period of cohabitation with Prime Minister Jospin] is to make sure, each in his place and with respect for the other, that we both serve the interests and the values that tran-scend our positions, that unite us and that quite simply are the ideas of the Republic. In the very first rank of these are equality of chances, public morality and Republican virtue.

Shortly before the legislative elections that imposed 'cohabitation' on Chirac, the first issue of a new weekly, *Marianne* (symbol of the Republic), appeared. The editor, J.-F. Kahn, explained its aims (*Le Monde*, 28 April 1997). The project, above all, was to be political. 'The title, *Marianne*, has programmatic value. It places the new weekly under the auspices of values that are lay, patriotic, democratic, humanist, social and liberal, in a word, Republican.'

Patrick Kessel, president of the Comité Laïcité République, invokes 'Marianne against Fascism' as the title of his article (referring to the shock of municipal election victories of Le Pen's *Front national* a few months before). In these moments of collective doubt, he argues, one must know how to find resources, not in a mythic image of the past, but by elaborating a modern form of hope: 'Republican values, which make freedom the measure of the man, secularity which provides the means, citizenship which is the form, these are today the only barrier against totalitarianism' in France and abroad (feature article in *Le Monde*, 13 February 1997).

The mayor of Vauvenargues, in the same region as the site of Le Pen's success when the extreme-Right party gained control of several towns, including the important city of Toulon, points out that economic conditions alone cannot explain such an ominous event. (This, however, is a thoughtful analysis, much less of an incantation.)

> Le Pen is not Hitler and the economic situation cannot be compared with that of 1929. But our contemporaries have lost their guide-posts. The moral values on which our Republic is based, those of solidarity and civic expression, are every day being altered by poverty, unemployment and violence, not to speak of corruption, which is publicized to excess.
>
> (Christian de Barbarin, *Le Monde*, 22 March 1997)

The then director of Air France, Christian Blanc, battling to restore economic health to the national carrier, also invokes Republican values for his cause. 'A man of the Left, for ethical reasons', according to an interview with *Paris Match* (24 April 1997), he is imbued with the 'values of the dignity of man, the struggle against injustice and support for the general interest'. Whatever his sense of struggle, he regards the current economic debate as totally artificial. 'I feel closer to those classed on the Right than on the Left.'

Even President Chirac's bold decision to end compulsory military service, announced at the end of May 1996, meets with 'Republican' opposition. The leader of the Communist deputies in the Assembly, Alain Bocquet, condemned it for 'burying Valmy' – the first decisive victory of the French Revolution over foreign invaders and French aristocrats! The Communist newspaper *L'Humanité* weighed in on 29 May 1996, declaring that the president was putting at risk one of the pillars of Republican order: 'A Republican order born in revolutionary torments, when the nation . . . conquered its sovereignty by the *levée en masse* against the professional armies of the princes. Nostalgia? No. Fashions change, but the democratic conception of defence remains a burning actuality.'

Finally, beyond ritual incantations, the appeal to Republican values may also inspire serious and penetrating analyses of politics and society. Lionel Jospin's endeavour to revive the ethical concerns of state and citizens is one example. Another is the solemn appeal by Charles Millon, then president of the UDF (Centre-Right) in the National Assembly, entitled

'*Refonder la République*', reported extensively in *Le Monde* (30 September 1994). Ironically, the validity of Millon's critique was amply confirmed by his own opportunistic behaviour, when he sacrificed his Republican principles for the sake of National Front votes following the March 1998 regional elections.

'We are facing, powerlessly, the degradation of the political situation', he begins. 'Politicians are being called to account, but institutions also risk contestation, and the Republic itself risks being disavowed.' In the eyes of the French, society is blocked and the Republic has been 'confiscated' – confiscated by the technocrats who, in the pursuit of efficiency, consider democracy a waste of time; confiscated by private interests; confiscated by elected members, who seek to profit from their mandates. (The idea of the Republican state as arbiter and protector, as François Furet puts it, has been emptied of its content because of the 'confiscation' of policy by the technocrats: 'United France . . . ', in Furet, Julliard and Rosanvallon, *La République du Centre*, 51).

The French, as a result, feel that the Republic has two levels of citizenship: the top level is guaranteed the privilege of being above the law; it gains from economic growth without suffering when there is a crisis. The lower level is that of people exposed to the effects of chance, who suffer from the anguish of unemployment and the sense of sacrifice unshared by others.

The remedy, Millon argues, is to reconcile the French with the Republic by rehabilitating politics, guaranteeing the separation of powers and restoring an active citizenship. The collective dimension of political renewal is precisely that of the general interest. But this 'compass of public action' is disturbed by the current confusion of roles and functions:

> While the experts wish to govern, the media to decide, the executive to legislate and the judges to moralize, there appears a multiplication of deputies–officials, ministers–party leaders and politicians–managers. It is time to put an end to this confusion before it becomes collusion.
>
> (*Le Monde*, 30 September 1994)

Accordingly, officials need first to choose between their established career and the risks of politics, as in Britain, and should not be able to combine the two. (French officials are entitled to join the advisory staffs of government ministers, or even take up political positions, without having to resign from the civil service. If their political party is defeated they may resume their original career.) This 'confusion' of politics and administration, as Millon rightly points out, affects the impartiality of the civil service. (In her study of the *grands corps*, M.-C. Kessler warns against the 'attraction of politics' for the civil service: *Les grands corps de l'Etat*, 72–4; and see my Chapter 6, 'Elites'.)

Second, in Millon's view, 'It is urgent to combat all doubtful proximity between the state apparatus and private interests, by eliminating the ambiguities of the mixed [public–private sector] economy and strictly controlling public works contracts.' Third, and clearly related to the above, the financing of electoral campaigns should also be reviewed. It follows, fourth, that the rigorous delimitation of state intervention and the definition of its essential missions are needed to eliminate certain 'grey' zones where corruption flourishes. Here Millon's recommendations are strongly supported by the definitive analysis of Yves Mény, *La corruption de la République*; and see also Chapter 8, 'Affairs'.

The integrity of politics also requires that ministers follow the coherent policies of government, Millon insists, and not allow their *cabinets* to take over the work of administration; nor should they let the 'technocratic aristocracy' dictate policy decisions according to their own criteria. Yet another 'urgent necessity' is to put an end to the 'Republican monarchy' by setting up real counter-powers to the excessive authority of the state. One of the characteristics of the 'French exception', Millon argues, is precisely its 'immoderate taste for the concentration of power, an instinctive reverence for power that is hardly transparent or under control, culminating in the notion of *raison d'Etat*.'

Even 'in the land of Montesquieu', he continues, parliamentary control of the executive is excessively undeveloped and the opposition, unlike the situation in Britain, has no real status. As for the other great counter-power, the judiciary, the cascade of 'affairs' implicating politicians should leave no doubt as to the real state of things. The independence of the judiciary should instead be guaranteed and the intervention of the minister of justice (i.e. in blocking or delaying prosecutions in 'sensitive' cases) should be strictly controlled by law. Here, as in the proposal to limit the *cumul des mandats* (where legislative and executive positions are held concurrently, for example a parliamentary deputy and mayor of a city), Millon's proposals anticipated the reforms inaugurated by the Jospin government three years later (see Chapters 7 and 8).

Everyone should understand, Millon concludes: 'It is a question of re-founding the Republic. The Republic, in the course of time, has lost its substance, has forgotten its *raison d'être*.' Its ideal is to guarantee the separation of powers and to supervise the dignity of the state and the integrity of those who serve it: instead, it confronts the hydra of corruption. Moreover, the Republic, which should restore social harmony and safeguard the equality of chances, instead offers the painful spectacle of 'exclusion' (that of the poor, the homeless, the unemployed: analysed in Chapter 12).

Indeed, Jospin's own critique indicates how much needs to be done. 'When the force of virtue ceases, the Republic is despoiled': Montesquieu.

References

Bouloiseau, M. (1972) *La République jacobine*, Paris: Seuil.

Flaubert, G. (1857) *Madame Bovary*.

Furet, F. (1988) 'La France unie . . . ' in F. Furet, J. Julliard and P. Rosanvallon, *La République du Centre*, Paris: Calmann-Lévy.

Hazareesingh, S. (1994) *Political Traditions in Modern France*, Oxford: Oxford University Press.

L'Humanité, 29 May 1996.

Kessler, M.-C. (1994) *Les grands corps de l'Etat*, Paris: PUF.

Madison, J. (1961) *The Federalist Papers*, intro. C. Rossiter, New York: New American Library.

Marianne, J.-F. Kahn (ed.).

Mayeur, J.-M. (1973) *Les débuts de la Troisième République*, Paris: Seuil.

Mény, Y. (1992) *La corruption de la République*, Paris: Fayard.

Le Monde, various.

Montesquieu, Ch. de S. (1748) *De l'esprit des lois*.

Rousseau, J.-J. (1762) *Du contrat social*.

Thomson, D. (1969) *Democracy in France since 1870*, London: Oxford University Press.

Vovelle, M. (1972) *La Chute de la monarchie*, Paris: Seuil.

5   Grandeur

> La France pouvait, dans ce sens, exercer une grande action, prendre une
> grande figure, servir grandement son intérêt et celui du genre humain.
>
> Charles de Gaulle

Virtue and power are united in Gaullist rhetoric. 'Grandeur' is certainly
considered specific to France – it evokes glorious memories of French
power and French prestige – but it also conveys a universal message: the
virtue of France's 'civilizing mission' throughout the world. Is such rhetoric
– reiterated by the neo-Gaullist Right – still another instance (as so often
with 'Republican values') of preferring ritual familiarity to the rigours of
the real world?

The notion of grandeur derives especially from the long reign of
Louis XIV, when French became the language of the elites in the 'civilized'
countries of Europe; from the extraordinary ambitions and achievements
of the Napoleonic era, when the 'universal' principles of the French
Revolution – liberty, equality, fraternity – implanted themselves in the
lands conquered by French arms; while even in the turmoil of the nineteenth century France was still – in envious German eyes – the *grande
nation* of the Western world.

Yet it was in reaction to the revival of German might – and the humiliation of France's defeat and occupation during the Second World War –
that de Gaulle was impelled to strive, above all, for grandeur: to efface the
treacherous experience of the recent past and to renew the sentiment of
French pride and honour.

The towering personality of de Gaulle was thus a major factor in the
pursuit of grandeur: by refusing the dependent status that France's pitiable
condition on the eve of liberation assumed; insisting (in vain) on equal
partnership with the superpowers; asserting the right to fully independent
views, even when contrary to the policy of France's great ally (withdrawal
from the integrated military structure of NATO; advocating neutrality for

South-East Asia – anathema to America, embroiled in the Vietnam war); constructing a new '*Europe des patries*', but excluding Britain, servile 'Anglo-Saxon' accomplice of the United States; indeed counterbalancing American power with the vision of Europe 'from the Atlantic to the Urals'.

Two major obstacles confronted – and confront – the pursuit of grandeur: the external environment, which France could influence but not control; and insufficient resources to sustain grandeur. It was a 'great-power' policy based on middle-power capacity.

It is not surprising that 'recalcitrant' external conditions – the disastrous campaign in Indochina, the demoralizing and divisive war in Algeria – should have created such problems for France, given that even the super-powers could neither foresee nor resolve a similar predicament: for America, the Vietnam war; for the Soviet Union, Afghanistan.

As for insufficient resources to sustain a policy of grandeur, France's ally, Britain, equally a nuclear-armed, permanent member of the UN Security Council, is an exemplary case. As early as 1947, soon after the end of the Second World War, the 'fuel crisis' in Britain forced the Attlee government to hand over 'responsibility' for the security of Greece and Turkey to the Americans. Hardly a decade later came the Suez fiasco (shared with France) when the would-be great powers were compelled to climb down in the face of the 'godfather's' displeasure: Britain's financial plight required American aid.

Pursuit of grandeur: external constraints: internal resources – the eternal triangle dominates four areas of major importance to France: Indochina and Algeria; the Atlantic alliance; Europe; ex-colonial Africa.

Already, de Gaulle's *Mémoires de guerre* (1944–6) presage the difficulties ahead. Referring to the three wars imposed on France by Germany, the Free French leader castigates the 'malevolence of the Anglo-Saxon powers' (p. 45) obliging a weakened France to renounce security guarantees from Germany after the First World War. During and after the Second World War, 'British ambition' seized the opportunities offered by a fluid situation to manoeuvre and extend its power in the Mediterranean region – at the expense of France (p. 54).

The Levant (Near East) was critical. The origin of the 'affair' was America's 'taste for hegemony', but the impulse came from Britain, exploiting its military success against Vichy forces in Syria and the Lebanon (French colonies) to take over from the French (pp. 181–3). Although, for de Gaulle, 'the honour and interest of our country are at stake' (p. 197), significantly he found little backing for his stand within France itself, whose politicians and diplomats sought to avoid a conflict with Britain. Crucially, moreover, de Gaulle failed to appreciate the strength of nationalist forces in Syria and Lebanon, striving for independence from France. Typically, an external scapegoat (here, Anglo-Saxon ambition) was found instead. The pattern was to be repeated, with devastating results, in South-East Asia and in North Africa.

Indochina and Algeria

Rarely was the mystique of French imperialism taken so far, records Jean-Pierre Rioux, than in the early postwar years. The Brazzaville conference on North Africa in January 1944 excluded any idea of autonomy or any possibility of change outside the French empire; not even self-government was envisaged. The French parliament remained the real legislative power. When a nationalist leader, Messali Hadj, was deported in May 1945 for demanding an Algerian government, riots broke out and a hundred Europeans were killed. The ensuing French repression was ferocious (the Sétif massacre): 6,000 to 8,000 Algerians lost their lives (Rioux, 127–33).

Meanwhile, in Indochina, nationalist movements had also developed during the war, especially in Vietnam. Early in 1945 Japanese troops arrested and disarmed the French forces loyal to Vichy. In August the Japanese themselves surrendered. The nationalist forces of the Viet Minh, led by the veteran Communist leader Ho Chi Minh, took over the country with extraordinary rapidity, the Vietnamese emperor even abdicating in their favour. To ensure the Japanese surrender, however, Allied forces intervened: Nationalist Chinese in the north, British in the south.

The stage was set for negotiations: Ho Chi Minh insisted on independence; the French demanded a return to colonial or protectorate status, within the shadowy orbit of a new 'French Union'. Agreement was reached in March 1946: the Viet Minh accepted the stationing of French troops in northern Vietnam (to be phased out in five years) in return for French recognition of the 'free state' of Vietnam, within the Union. General Leclerc, hero of the liberation of France, realized that with the limited means available it would be impossible to fight the Viet Minh and regain control of the country.

These views were not shared by the French High Commissioner, Admiral d'Argenlieu, an enthusiastic supporter of de Gaulle and a man 'imbued with the traditions of French grandeur'. D'Argenlieu, convinced that the leaders of the Viet Minh were no more than Communist agitators, complained to the future French commander in Vietnam, General Valluy, that he was 'astonished that France has such a fine expeditionary corps in Indo-China and yet its leaders prefer to negotiate rather than fight' (cited by Philippe Devillers, *Histoire du Viet-Nam*, 149, 340–1; Devillers was a member of Leclerc's staff).

Returning to France, d'Argenlieu sounded the alarm that if Indochina were lost, the whole French Union would be threatened. This prediction had its effect on French deputies who were haunted by the spectre of France's weakness – political, military and financial. In their view, France could only assert its authority by standing up to the Viet Minh: by 'teaching it a hard lesson', as General Valluy proclaimed, before the French bombarded Haiphong in November 1946. Several thousands lost their lives. The '*sale guerre*' began.

When the French forces, defeated at Dien Bien Phu, withdrew from Indochina as a result of the Geneva agreements negotiated by Mendès France in 1954, French North Africa was already in a state of crisis. In November 1954, Algerian nationalists, frustrated by French intransigence, launched a series of attacks in which a French teacher was killed. Sending armed reinforcements, Mendès France insisted: 'One does not compromise when it comes to defending the internal peace of the nation [Algerian departments were considered part of France] and the integrity of the Republic.' His interior minister, François Mitterrand, affirmed: 'Algeria is France. From Flanders to the Congo there is the law, there is only one nation, only one parliament. That is the Constitution and that is our will' (Rioux, 66–7).

The Socialist deputy, Naegelen, later to be governor of Algeria, for his part declared: 'Let us not deceive ourselves, to lose North Africa is to lose, in a short time, the whole of Africa and then the French Union.' The result, he went on, would be for France to 'fall to the rank of a secondary power and even a vassal. It is not only our prestige that is at stake but our national independence.'

The infernal cycle of terrorism and repression took over. A year later, the Algerian National Liberation Front launched its general insurrection. The French response was like that of the Americans in Vietnam: 'Pacification first, reforms later' (Rioux, 82–3).

Now de Gaulle himself was in the political wilderness – *la traversée du désert* – between 1946 and 1958. But although sympathetic to *l'Algérie française*, he came to realize that the unending war, despite French military victories (accompanied by torture), was dividing France, was creating anxiety among the million European *colons* (settlers) that they would be abandoned, was producing dissension in the army as well as increasing distrust of the paralysed party system and its ephemeral governments and, above all, was a burden (military, political, economic and psychological) on France that rendered impossible any sustained pursuit of grandeur.

When de Gaulle was called upon by the French coalition government, at the end of its tether in 1958, to save France from the threat of civil war, the 'man of destiny' manoeuvred with brilliance between the various contending forces, appearing to support each side in turn, but always moving forward to the inevitable decision: first the 'peace of the brave' and then, in 1962, when it was obvious that the Algerian nationalists would not compromise, independence.

Atlantic alliance

Was de Gaulle's 'grand design' to play a major role in the world compatible with the real situation of France?, asks the historian Serge Berstein. Moreover, could one envisage an autonomous French policy apart from the Atlantic alliance, given that French security in the Cold War depended upon the American nuclear umbrella? These tensions, if not contradictions, of 'grandeur', while much attenuated under subsequent presidents, are still evident today.

In the 1960s, however, de Gaulle, released from the agonizing crisis of Algeria (followed by successful decolonization of black Africa), felt free to challenge what he regarded as American 'hegemony' impinging on the 'national sovereignty' of France. Even though he had previously supported the Fourth Republic's acceptance of NATO strategy, he became increasingly critical (once in power) of America's unilateral decisions. Fundamentally, de Gaulle rejected the claims of the superpowers to dominate world affairs.

On the one hand, de Gaulle's withdrawal in 1963 from the integrated military command structure of NATO symbolized his insistence on an autonomous status for France, which would then freely dispose of its support (indeed, de Gaulle vigorously backed the Americans in subsequent Cold War crises). On the other hand, de Gaulle promoted an alternative foreign policy separate from the two power-blocs: thus, advocacy of a neutral South-East Asia at a time when the United States was committed to the Vietnam war; the visionary proposal of a Europe from the Atlantic to the Urals (i.e. including European Russia); efforts to achieve a special relationship with Soviet leaders (counterbalancing what de Gaulle saw as Anglo-Saxon hegemony in NATO); and the drive to stimulate cultural, and even political, independence of the two power-blocs in Latin America and North America (sensationally demonstrated by de Gaulle's 'separatist' provocation while on a visit to Canada: 'Vive le Québec libre!'). A pale reflection of de Gaulle's crusade was President Chirac's own journey to Latin America in 1997: in the absence of weighty economic ties, Chirac's discourse could do little more than stress the value of 'latin' culture.

Significantly for the future role of France in world affairs, it was not just American but French public opinion which no longer felt able to endorse the general's ambition for grandeur. According to French public opinion polls, 1967 marked a turning point in what had previously been massive support. In January 1968, while opinion was almost equally divided on whether France had the means to practise an independent policy, 42 per cent (against 28 per cent) judged that independence did not extend to the military sphere and 47 per cent (against 26 per cent) considered that it did not apply in economic matters (Berstein, 261–3).

Jacques Chirac, neo-Gaullist president of France, had sufficiently regressed from de Gaulle's peremptory stance as to declare in 1995 that France would rejoin the military committee of NATO – provided that certain military positions would be made available to European officers, including the head of NATO's southern command. The United States, considering that France did not possess the requisite naval power, refused. Even France's ally, the German minister of defence, would not support France's claim. In a public statement in October 1997, he said that France was 'isolated' in NATO and should rejoin the military committee. (Yet another ill-considered initiative by Chirac, the resumption of nuclear testing, met strong opposition, within Europe and especially in Australia and Japan, and turned into a fiasco.)

Europe

Indeed, de Gaulle's European policy experienced a similar disavowal. The general's concept was that of '*Europe des patries*' – a partnership of nations, not a federal structure – and it was based on the hegemony of the two leading powers, France and Germany. As such, it necessarily excluded Britain, considered to be the Trojan Horse of American influence inside Europe (Berstein, 249).

De Gaulle's dark suspicions of Anglo-Saxon designs in 1963 – his first rejection of British entry – were strikingly revealed (much later) by his confidant, Alain Peyrefitte. 'The Anglo-Saxons', according to the general, want a Europe that 'has no longer the ambition to be itself'. They want an American Europe,

> the Europe of the multinationals. A Europe which, in its economy, and still more in its defence and in its politics, would be placed under an inexorable American hegemony. A Europe in which every European country, starting with our own, would lose its soul.
>
> (quoted in *Histoire Term*, 325)

It was the general's successor, President Pompidou, who if not abandoning de Gaulle's ambitions modified them in accordance with greater realism. For Pompidou (who had 'saved' de Gaulle from the 'events' of 1968) realized that Germany was now the dominant economic power in

Europe, and that it would be advisable for France to balance that power with the aid of British entry into the Common Market.

The complexity of the resulting French approach to the European Community, Anne Stevens explains, is that it includes elements of Jean Monnet's vision of the logic of greater European co-operation and of Gaullist rhetoric. Each successive president since 1958 has encouraged progress in certain areas. For de Gaulle, the Common Agricultural Policy (benefiting especially French farmers) and the customs union were the key economic factors. Pompidou, besides enlarging the Community, moved towards economic and monetary union. The partnership between President Giscard d'Estaing and Chancellor Helmut Schmidt of Germany then developed such important initiatives as the European monetary system and the mechanism for political co-operation. President Mitterrand, too, was a convinced European; even though his 'political' referendum on adhesion to the Maastricht Treaty (intended to divide the opposition) nearly proved fatal (Stevens, *The Government and Politics of France*, 311–17).

Jospin, too, maintained the European policy of his predecessors. Despite the failure of the 1997 Amsterdam summit to agree on three major issues – development of a common foreign and security policy; elaboration of European judiciary and police co-operation; and institutional expansion of the European Union to include countries of Eastern Europe – the Socialist government strongly supported the programme to achieve a single European currency (the Euro) in accordance with Jospin's proclaimed 'realism of the Left', that is, economic orthodoxy (see Chapter 7, 'Parties').

Administratively, as Jean Charlot points out, French high officials have responded reasonably well to the European challenge, according to the system of government *à la française*: that is, 'centralized decision-making of an enarcho-political nature' (*énarchie* refers to rule by graduates of the ENA). French representatives are considered good negotiators; but the main French weakness is too statist and hierarchical a conception of the Community (Charlot, *La politique en France*, 58–9).

Stevens is even more forthright in her conclusion. French response to the European Community, she argues (p. 327), 'illustrates the combination of ideological rhetoric and pragmatic, almost opportunistic, management that tends to constitute the formulation of policy'. It is a combination that operates within a fragmented political and administrative system, which is legally and formally rational and highly structured, but in fact works through complex and interlocking informal relationships. (Such is the characteristic of French elitism, which will be examined in the next chapter.)

Africa

The former French (and Belgian) colonies of North and black Africa are the last sphere for the projection of grandeur. During the Cold War, France was considered responsible for the security of this area, just as the United States was the gendarme for the rest of the 'free world'.

Even after the Cold War, France still retained its military pacts with favoured (or endangered) African states, its oligarchic alliances and its 'networks' of informal, especially economic, relationships between French politicians and senior officials and their African counterparts.

But the 'wind of change', which had brought independence (but not democracy, for the most part) to the former colonies in the 1960s, blew in certain areas into a hurricane of violence and bloodshed in subsequent years. In the grand tradition of the Foreign Legion, French forces advanced from remote outposts to save embattled clients. The French military establishment, the secret services, the aid missions, the enterprising businessmen, the networks of clientalist relations, were intimately involved in safeguarding established regimes, whatever their reputation for democracy or autocracy, stability or disorder, economic growth or decline, public integrity or corruption – usually the latter.

France has defence agreements with eight African states and economic co-operation and military assistance agreements with more than twenty African states. These agreements do not authorize the intervention of French forces to maintain internal order; but the situation on the ground is much more ambiguous.

There is a 'delicate frontier between sovereignty and intervention', reported J.-P. Langellier.

> To get involved or not? To interfere or leave things alone? For more than thirty years, every time a serious crisis erupts in France's 'preserve' in Africa there is always the same dilemma. Should one remain deaf to the appeal for help from the leader in power, and refuse to assist a friendly regime that is in danger? Or should one, on the contrary, help the leader to regain control and thereby anger the forces of opposition? . . . Almost always France decides to act. It acts like a gendarme but, more and more often, despite itself.
>
> (*Le Monde*, 30 May 1996)

If France is resolved to intervene, Langellier continues, it is because it knows (thanks to its 8,000 troops) that it can influence events. 'Africa is the only continent still within the reach of French power', said Louis de Guiringaud twenty years ago. 'It is the only one where, with 500 men, one can change the course of history' – grandeur indeed! Thus, since 1964, when France restored the president of Gabon to power, France has not ceased to intervene in independent Africa, once every two years on average.

The turning point came in April 1994 with the genocide of the Tutsi minority (and moderate Hutus) by Hutu extremists in Rwanda, former Belgian colony, later within France's zone of influence. France had a military assistance agreement with Rwanda and, until the slaughter began, was actively engaged in boosting the strength of the Hutu-led armed forces. (Indeed, according to a series of reports in *Le Figaro* from 12 January 1998, French arms were still being delivered even after the massacre had begun, although this was officially denied.) After Tutsi exiles from the English-speaking neighbouring countries (an important point!) drove out the Hutu army, French forces intervened to establish what they called a 'humanitarian zone' free from military attack. That protected zone did save many Hutus from reprisals, but it also protected those among the Hutu 'militia' who had been most viciously engaged in killing Tutsis, and who were allowed to escape into Zaire.

Even though, in an extraordinary reversal of fortune, the Tutsis' allies in Zaire (fighting against Mobutu's oppressive regime), aided by Uganda and the new Tutsi-led government in Rwanda, proceeded on their conquering path, in turn committing atrocities, the French government still backed its old clients by appealing for an international conference – on humanitarian grounds – that would block the Tutsi 'rebel' advance.

Isolated internationally, unable to influence the course of events, the French (Chirac–Juppé) government fell back on the familiar Anglo-Saxon bogey: the Anglophone countries of central Africa, supported by the United States, were intent on eliminating French influence in this vital area. The Uganda–Rwanda–Burundi axis, according to *Le Monde*'s analysis of 2–3 February 1997, is 'primordial for the United States'. Uganda, 'America's aircraft carrier in the heart of Africa', watches over the Sudan, with its rebellions and Muslims, to the North; Ethiopia and Eritrea to the East, 'with strategic access to the Red Sea'; and those provinces of Zaire that are 'so full of [mineral] wealth'. (American reaction, reported by the newspaper on 29 April 1997, was that the suggestion of an 'American plot' bordered on paranoia.)

As for France, according to *Le Monde*'s officially inspired report (2–3 February 1997), it 'has never deviated from its attachment to the integrity and stability of Zaire, a country it considers the key to the whole of central Africa'. France

> still believes that Marshal Mobutu can play a positive role for his country: to use his aura as veteran African chief to re-establish a

semblance of order, to revive political life, to restructure the army, re-conquer the lost territories [gained by the 'rebels'], organize presidential and legislative elections, carry out the electoral campaign, be elected and at last favour the true transition to democracy to which the country aspires.

Astonishing! Here was the man, known for his rapacity and corruption for more than thirty years, the man whose ill-paid, disorganized and demoralized army had fled, time after time, without putting up a fight (except when robbing and killing civilians), the man who had manoeuvred and intrigued in order to sabotage any move towards democracy, the man who was the fundamental obstacle to reform: here he was, presented as the leader worthy of international support! (See *Le Monde* three months later: 'The True History of Marshal Mobutu, who built up a fortune of 4 billion dollars by robbing his country', with details, 18–19 May 1997.)

No wonder that a French specialist, Jean-François Bayart, director of the Centre d'études et de recherches internationales, should reply in answer to the question: 'Is Africa today "sick" of France?' (*Le Monde*, 29 April 1997). This is not a question of pathology.

> It is because we claimed that Mobutu was the final guarantor of the unity of Zaire, that he was the last barrier against chaos – of which he was in fact the organizer, although we did not want to see it – so we supported him to the end . . . .On the contrary, France is sick of Africa. We were accomplices, in Rwanda, in the preparation of geno-cide. We organized, even financed, the sending to Zaire of Serb war criminals as mercenaries to defend one of the most deplorable dicta-torships of the Cold War.

But is it now possible, after the death of Jacques Foccart (de Gaulle's adviser on Africa, famous for his 'networks') and with the collapse of Mobutu, that France can overcome the failure of its strategy in central Africa and develop a new policy? Bayart doubted it, because 'the French political class, whatever its alignment, considers foccartism to be the appro-priate way of understanding French-African relations, giving primacy to the policy of networks and a mix of para-diplomatic action and private affairs'. Thus it is improbable, he considered, that France would give up 'foccartism', even though it was responsible for the fiasco of France's African policy.

It is up to the Jospin government to disprove this gloomy prediction. In principle, as Foreign Affairs Minister Hubert Védrine proposed on 24 June 1997, France is seeking a 'balance' between its responsibilities in Africa and the desire not to get involved in internal issues. But such has always been the case. All the same, Védrine insists that France needs to revise its methods and the way it uses its influence: French networks in Africa 'belong to another era'.

Does such an avowal mark the end of Gaullist grandeur? Not for the populist champion of the Right, Charles Pasqua, tough minister of the interior in the Balladur government of the mid-1990s, former opponent of the Maastricht Treaty and expert manipulator of networks. In his rallying call to the faithful ('Address to my Companions', *Le Monde*, 21 October 1997) Pasqua claimed that 'the principles defined by General de Gaulle' reappear, in France's present predicament, as the most modern that can be found. These are the principles: 'the reality of nations, the right of peoples, the refusal of hegemonies, participation, the promises of Francophonie [French-speaking countries]'. But what, in substance rather than rhetoric, do they mean? The 'reality of nations': back to *l'Europe des patries*? The 'right of peoples' to do what? 'Participation' how? 'Refusal of hegemonies' – in Europe, the Atlantic pact, the international economy – in what way? As for Francophonie, its 'promises'? Simply to pose these questions suggests that nostalgia for the Gaullist past is no substitute for policies related to the present. As for Pasqua's past: the age of *political* networks, for France acting on its own in the world, is over: the age of *economic* interdependence has begun.

References

Berstein, S. (1989) *La France de l'expansion*, vol. 1, Paris: Seuil.

Charlot, J. (1994) *La politique en France*, Paris: Fallois.

Devillers, Ph. (1952) *Histoire du Viet-Nam de 1940 à1952*, Paris: Seuil.

Gaulle, Ch. de (1959) *Mémoires de guerre – Le Salut*, Paris: Plon.

Histoire Term (1995) coll. J. Marseille, Paris: Nathan.

Le Monde, various.

Rioux, J.-P. (1980, 1983) *La France de la Quatrième République*, Paris: vol. 1, vol. 2, Seuil.

Stevens, A. (1996) *The Government and Politics of France*, London: Macmillan.

Part II

Politics

There are two characteristic features of the political system, in one sense complementary, in another, contradictory:

The first follows the general trend in all the 'developed' countries of *convergence* towards global economic norms: hence the adaptation of the political system to economic imperatives.

The second relates to the *specificity* of politics and society in individual countries: here the role of politics (with civil society) is to express national and group identities; above all, the sense of belonging to a significant community, class, region or nation, which is identified for members as much by what it is not (the 'other') as by its own inherent interests and values.

Thus, Jean Charlot has shown how the French 'Right' and 'Left' identify with particular values in a list of twenty-four politically and symbolically 'charged' words. 'Liberty' is the only word they have in common. Otherwise the Left most prefers social protection, followed by tolerance, rights of man, liberty, equality, Europe, participation, change and culture. The Right, on the other hand, prefers security, followed by enterprise, order, property, progress, *patrie*, religion, rigour, nation, (economic) liberalism, competition and liberty (1992 survey cited by Charlot, *La politique en France*, 44).

All the above may be described as 'Republican values', but clearly there is a very different emphasis from Right to Left, reflecting different economic interests and varying conceptions of society and politics. At the same time, despite these 'specificities', there is evidently a convergence among the major political parties on economic issues: the differences being more about the means to achieve a desired end (the Maastricht criteria for a single currency, for example) than the ends themselves. (Note the acid comments by Jacques Julliard on

'Centrism', as a continuous web of complicities and networks, producing a consensus based on economic modernism and 'democratic' elitism: 'The Journey to the Centre', in Furet, Julliard and Rosanvallon, *La République du Centre*, 110–12.)

And yet these political 'differences', because they are rooted in membership of particular communities, groups or classes, cannot be taken for granted by the political and economic elites – elites which are the main motive force for convergence towards European and international norms. Social and economic differences come out clearly in the responses to the referendum organized by President Mitterrand in 1992, on the issue of ratifying the Maastricht treaty. The 51 per cent who voted 'yes' did so for three main reasons: to assure a lasting peace in Europe, to continue constructing 'Europe', and to compete more effectively against Japan and the United States. The 49 per cent who voted 'no', on the other hand, emphasized that support for Maastricht would mean loss of sovereignty for France; they refused 'to leave France in the hands of the Brussels technocrats' (Charlot, 51).

Significant differences also emerge from surveys carried out by the European Community. Thus, 17 per cent of French people over 15 years of age were 'very afraid' of the effect of the enlarged market, against 10 per cent who were 'very hopeful'. The main fears were – and are – more unemployment, less job creation, 'loss of our national identity' and 'too much immigration' – all salient factors in the formation of a particular 'identity'. The main hopes were 'more jobs and less unemployment' (precisely contrary to the fearful), more effective competition with the United States and Japan, easier commercial exchanges and the possibility of working anywhere in the European Community.

Fears, as Charlot points out (p. 52), reflect the pessimistic outlook of the less educated and less qualified in face of modernization, opening to Europe and the world, and hence intensified competition. Hopes, on the other hand, represent the optimistic outlook of the more educated and socially mobile. (There is, of course, an even greater division of opinion – between fears and hopes – in Britain where the majority of Conservatives, contrary to the situation in France, are 'Eurosceptics'.)

Such, then, are the related aspects of the convergence–specificity theme. First, the role of the elites, which is identified (as noted above) with European and international 'convergence'. This unusually closed circle of elites – administrative, political and economic – seen as aloof and arrogant, has come under increasing criticism for its failure to solve problems affecting ordinary people (high rate of unemployment, 'exclusion', precarious job outlook, crime and 'insecurity'). See Chapter 6.

Second, the intermediary role of political parties, operating between the citizens and the state, which imparts legitimacy to the system, in accordance with democratic theory. No less important, however, is the (unavowed) intermediary role of political parties, relating business interests to political decisions, thus acting as a transmission belt between wealth and power. See Chapter 7.

Third, related to the above is the tendency to corruption. The notorious 'affairs' of the 1980s, extending into the 1990s and affecting political parties of the Right and the Left, demonstrate the 'excessive' aspect of a wide-ranging collusive relationship. For in the practice of democracy – as distinct from its 'pure' theory – the interests of business have priority. To act otherwise is to risk economic collapse and, with it, political and social chaos.

For this reason, in politics the general aim of 'convergence' is to facilitate the progress of capitalism: to adapt the political system to economic imperatives. The 'specific' task of politicians, on the other hand, is to attend to the demands of citizens, without the latter upsetting the former (economic interests). See Chapters 7 and 8.

Fourth, largely in reaction to the above, is the importance of civil society. Civil society denotes those 'intermediate' groups and associations – asserting their autonomy from both the state and the economy – which (ideally) transform particular interests, whether environmental, feminist, generational, professional or intellectual, into the general interest: that is, the voice of citizens. A mature and effective civil society is the necessary counterpart both to the imperatives of market capitalism and to the exigencies of the state. See Chapter 9.

6 Elites

Plus que jamais, il me fallait donc prendre appui dans le peuple plutôt que dans les 'élites' qui, entre lui et moi, tendaient à s'interposer.

Charles de Gaulle

De Gaulle's belief in the legitimacy of his own direct relationship, through election, with the people – as distinct from the indirect 'representation' of the people by politicians, dependent upon a hierarchical structure of authority – illustrates the ambiguous situation of the elites. On the one hand, the formation of technocratic and administrative elites, issuing from the foundation by de Gaulle and his loyal minister, Michel Debré, of the Ecole national d'administration, was considered essential for the postwar reconstruction of France. On the other hand, the same elitist hierarchy could not but jeopardize that direct relationship with the people that de Gaulle so much cherished.

That same ambiguity persists today – for the elite is omnipresent – but with one important difference: in contrast to the years of economic growth, *les Trente Glorieuses*, France is now subject to a much more uncertain cycle of booms and slumps, resulting in a current high rate of unemployment and precarious prospects – for which the elite, even if still convinced of its own superiority, seems to have no solution. Jacques Chirac, wearing his Gaullist mantle during his successful presidential campaign, made the point by denouncing in 1995 the 'social fracture' in France between unresponsive elites and discontented people. The incoming president then widened the social divide, though he did not acknowledge this, by appointing his close aide, Alain Juppé, as prime minister – the elite of the elite!

It is hardly surprising that Juppé, ignominiously dismissed by his master during the 1997 legislative elections (but which failed to save the Right), should have come in for virulent criticism, precisely as the typically arrogant chief of the technocratic elite. Consider the acid portrait of Juppé by

Denis Jeambar, editor of the influential weekly *L'Express*: from his first days as prime minister, he showed the defects that would finish him: 'an unlimited ambition that tolerates no rival, an absolute incapacity to show any greatness of spirit, an autocratic temperament that stifles all generosity, a scornful behaviour that arouses violent reactions'.

Juppé and his henchmen (his director of *cabinet* and the secretary-general of the presidency), Jeambar went on,

> believe that they are invincible, that an election can always be won, that an opinion can be reversed, that the press can be manipulated, that power is not to be shared . . . .They believe in their masters (the president), but they also believe they have become masters.
>
> (Jeambar, *Un Secret d'Etat*, quoted by Gérard Courtois,
> *Le Monde des livres*, 4 July 1997)

It is precisely the conspicuous presence of the elites, in the highest official posts, among leading politicians and directing the most important enterprises, that makes them an easy target for criticism – when things go wrong. The extraordinary failures attributed to certain of these elites – the folly of the former head of Crédit lyonnais, for example – tend to discredit not just the individual, but the elitist system as such.

What is that system? And to what extent are the elites responsible for the 'social fracture' in France? Given the extent of shortcomings, what remedies have been suggested? To answer these questions requires an investigation of four major areas: the economic, political and administrative network of elites; the politicization of high officials and the confusion of roles; the combination of legislative and executive powers in the hands of politicians; and the critique of the *énarchie* and its implications for society.

Economic contrasts

A striking illustration of French elitism at work is the comparison by two French researchers, Bénedicte Bertin-Mourot and Michel Bauer, of the careers of directors of large firms in France and Germany. Their analysis of the heads of the 200 biggest enterprises in each country indicates two very different models of the production of elites. Their conclusion (in 1992) is that the French model, in terms both of economic efficiency in a competitive environment and of socio-economic effects, is a 'real handicap'.

The difference, in effect, is between 'directorial' and 'managerial' capitalism. Thus, the typical French director is a graduate of the *grandes écoles* and emerges from one of the *grands corps* (Mines, Inspectorate of Finances, Court of Accounts, Conseil d'Etat, etc.). He has no experience of the world of business, except what is acquired much later, and is 'catapulted' to the head of a firm which he directs without ever going through the various intermediate levels.

The typical head of a German enterprise, by contrast, certainly has a diploma, but starts his professional life in a firm and works his way up, practising different jobs and especially through apprenticeship improving his qualifications. Except in the distributive sector, where family firms dominate in both countries, all the other sectors – industry, services, banking – reveal the same difference between the 'directorial' and 'managerial' approach. The proportion of heads of enterprise coming from service to the state is six times higher in France than in Germany.

Two of the *grandes écoles* (Polytechnique and ENA) produce more than 45 per cent of the heads of firms surveyed; three (with the commercial school HEC) produce more than half. In comparison, none of the German establishments has such strength. In fact, more than a quarter of the directors of the biggest firms emerge by way of apprenticeship. Finally, while more than 70 per cent of German directors began their work as mid-level manager or below, this was the case with only 30 per cent in France.

The two researchers suggest that France is handicapped as a result of its elitism in three major ways. First, by restricting intake to those 'selected' by a narrow form of higher education and by service of the state, French firms lose out on the possibility of discovering an 'exceptional' entrepreneur. Second, the poor understanding of the firm often shown by French elites 'catapulted' into the top job, or 'parachuted' into senior positions, increases the hierarchical gap between the 'number one' and the rest of the staff. (The German director, who has worked his way up, has far more concrete knowledge of the firm and has closer and more personal relations with his staff, producing a more forceful and cohesive establishment.) Third and finally, the French version performs much less well in terms of motivation. A German senior executive knows that he has a good chance of eventually reaching the top; this is not the case in France, where the school and not work experience determines careers (Bertin-Mourot and Bauer, *Les 200 en France et en Allemagne*, quoted by Eric Izraelewicz, *Le Monde*, 20 May 1992).

Five years later, according to statistics reported by Yves Mamou (*Le Monde*, 9 September 1997), 43 per cent of the 200 largest French firms were headed by members of the *grands corps*, 31 per cent by those who owned the company and only 26 per cent by managers promoted within the firm.

Elite networks and politicization

A British former civil servant, Anne Stevens, also brings to bear a valuable comparative perspective. She emphasizes the 'closely interlocking
nature of the [French] elite which occupies the senior posts in every
branch of activity – politics, the civil service, public enterprise, the big
private companies, the media'. In 1989, twenty-one of the fifty leading
companies were headed by graduates from the Polytechnique. The interlocking network of elites, narrowly based, 'is often underpinned by social
contacts, family relationships and marital connections' (Stevens, 155–6).
As for the elitist hold on political power, M.-C. Kessler reports that in
1993 there were thirty-four deputies, eleven senators and seven ministers
in the government who were all graduates of the ENA (*Les grands corps de
l'Etat*, 106).

The system of ministerial advisory staffs or *cabinets* both expresses and
reinforces French elitism. Up to ten members of a *cabinet* are allowed for
senior government ministers and three to five for junior ministers. But
since the salaries proposed are small, ministers need to seek official and
unofficial members whose salaries can be met from other sources, as in the
case of officials. A further reason for the predominance of seconded officials is the need for expertise in the work of government departments:
thus, officials represented some 80 to 90 per cent of cabinet strength in the
1970s and even 70 per cent when the Socialists, employing more of their
own advisers, came to power in the 1980s. Moreover, the very senior
directeurs de cabinet were almost exclusively high officials in the period of the
Mauroy government, 1981–4 (Stevens, 129–30).

The fusion of political and administrative elites was at its height in the
Gaullist era. As many as one-third of government ministers at the end of
the 1960s were senior civil servants (compared to 12 per cent under the
Fourth Republic). Almost half the Gaullist ministers had passed the
entrance examination for teachers of secondary or higher education or for
entry to the ENA or Polytechnique (Berstein, vol. 1 205).

Further extending the scope of elite networks is the transfer of political
personalities and high officials into the economic sector – not just public
enterprises but also into the largest private (often former nationalized)
industries or into banking and insurance. Pierre Birnbaum, *Les Sommets de
l'Etat: essai sur l'élite du pouvoir en France* (1977), calculates that more than half
the ministers who left politics had joined the boards of enterprises. As
many as 28 per cent of high officials went into private sector firms, usually
in key positions. This extension of elite influence, Berstein notes, does not
so much represent the real social 'promotion' of socially mobile
newcomers as

the passage through new meritocratic channels of sons and daughters of the traditional leading class who, in addition to their assets of birth and wealth, bring competence and cultural inheritance, allowing them to play the most important part in the new circuits of social domination.
(Berstein, vol. 1 205–6; see also Wright, 111–13; Mény, 110–13)

Indeed, a noted scholar of the French educational system concludes that the educational reforms seeking to assure 'equality of chances' have actually 'organized the recruitment of the scholarly elite from members of the social elite' (A. Prost, quoted by Berstein and Rioux, vol. 2 235–7; and discussion in Chapter 3).

Accumulation of powers

Yet another French 'specificity' – the accumulation of legislative and executive functions in the same hands: *le cumul des mandats* – has been incisively analysed by Yves Mény in his book, *La corruption de la République* (and see my Chapter 8, 'Affairs'). The origins of this practice, conducive to the collusion of wealth and power and, in certain cases, to corruption, stems from the weakness of the French party system during the early years of the Republic. Political parties, unable to implant themselves effectively, were transformed into 'conglomerates of notables instead of organizations to mobilize the masses'. It was not the parties that selected the elites, but the elites that selected the parties (Mény, 68).

Similarly, when de Gaulle was propelled to power in 1958, his movement lacked an effective power-base: to neutralize the existing party networks the Gaullist movement co-opted local 'notables' who were prepared to 'accumulate' such positions concurrently with being elected deputies to the National Assembly. There was an extraordinary growth in the *cumul des mandats* – a phenomenon almost unknown elsewhere in Europe. Thus, while only one-third of deputies had a local mandate in the last years of the Third Republic, the proportion rose to 42 per cent under the Fourth. But by 1968 two-thirds had 'accumulated', and 96 per cent twenty years later! (Mény, 70–3).

There are two major consequences of the system of *cumuls*. The first is the fusion of executive powers exercised by the local elite – by the elected mayor of a city for example – and the legislative duties of the deputy at the national level. The deputy votes on legislation that may affect the activities of the mayor; the mayor then decides on extensive public works contracts for his or her town or city. The possibility of a conflict of interest is evident.

The second factor is that one person cannot effectively be both a full-time deputy and mayor of an important city. (Alain Juppé, for example, was both prime minister under Chirac and mayor of Bordeaux, one of France's largest cities; Chirac himself was for many years a deputy, and at times prime minister, while being mayor of Paris.) The practical consequence is that the deputy or minister looks after national affairs, while his *cabinet* does the local work. But the deputy is at least elected to that position, while members of his *cabinet*, with important de facto powers, are not: they are personal appointees, part of a clientalist network. (But note the proposals for reform discussed in Chapter 7.)

Thus, the fusion of powers under the system of *cumuls*, the transfer of expenditure on public works projects to local authorities under the decentralization programme (considered in Chapter 2) and the personalized networks linking politicians and notables to loyal followers: all these, as Mény and others have pointed out, are conducive to arbitrary decisions, if not worse. In Mény's critique:

> Privilege is substituted for law, particularist exchanges for general rules, a secretive oligarchy for open markets. Gradually there spreads the conviction, among the elites at first and then more widely, that everything can be exchanged, bought, arranged; that the holders of public authority can profit from their powers . . . .In short, an unhealthy climate, mixing corrupt affairs and privileges of all kinds, is formed . . . .Then the whole political system is affected, for it lacks the civic virtue dear to Montesquieu: indifference, rejection, anomie take the place of participation and defence of ideals and open the way to unpredictable events.
>
> (317–18)

Mény's criticism has been echoed by a noted American specialist on French elites, Ezra Suleiman. In *France: The Transformation of a Society*, translated into French in 1995, Suleiman contrasts postwar modernization, in which the elites played such a positive part, and the current situation of the state assailed by associations and lobbies of all sorts. The elites, he writes, no longer serve the state but make use of it to gain money and maintain their privileges. Corruption, however, is only the most visible part of the problems that need reform. For even the Left, when in power in the 1980s, did little or nothing. To the contrary, it granted legitimacy as never before to the institutions of the elite: the ENA, *grandes écoles, grands corps*.

Note that Suleiman's earlier analysis, *Elites in French Society* (1978), discussed in Chapter 3, appeared in the same year as Marie-Christine Kessler's study, *La politique de la haute fonction publique*, followed in 1986 by *Les grands corps de l'Etat*. The elite has been the target of criticism for years – of which the section that follows is only the most recent example – without its characteristic selection, formation and progression being substantially changed.

Critique of the *énarchie*

In a critical situation, when public institutions are discredited for failing to live up to their principles and, just as important, failing to solve the practical problems of ordinary people, there is always a tendency for one section of the elite to try to save itself by turning against the other. Hence the spate of criticism by leading politicians, during the vital legislative elections of May–June 1997, of the *'énarchie'* – an obvious scapegoat for the failings of the elite in general.

As Guy Berger, president of the association of former pupils of the ENA, complained after the elections, there had been a 'campaign of denigration' by the politicians: the Socialist Laurent Fabius, former prime minister, had proposed to suppress the ENA; Denis Tillinac, close to Chirac, had castigated the *'énarques'*; Alain Juppé, then prime minister, spoke of replacing the ENA with something else; and Alain Madelin, standard-bearer of 'neo-liberal' economics, naughtily suggested that Ireland had its IRA, Italy had its Mafia, 'and France has its ENA' (reported by Rafaële Rivais, *Le Monde*, 25 June 1997).

The president of the ENA association, however, was satisfied with the statement of the new prime minister, Lionel Jospin, supporting the public service but urging principled reform. He might well be satisfied: nine of Jospin's ministers and twenty directors of ministerial *cabinets* were graduates of the ENA! Jospin's one-third of ministers issued from the ENA compares more than favourably with the 20 per cent registered by the Messmer government in 1972, the same proportion for Raymond Barre in 1978 and Pierre Mauroy in 1981; and one-quarter for Balladur in 1993 and Juppé in 1995 (but a high spot for Chirac in 1986, with 45 per cent). As for the directors of *cabinets* in the Jospin government, the proportion of ENA graduates was one of the highest in years: 74 per cent (R. Rivais, quoting François Kesler, former deputy director of ENA: *Le Monde*, 27 June 1997).

More disinterested and substantial criticism of the ENA comes from other sources than the political class. Pupils of the ENA themselves criticize the overly conformist teaching of the school, intended to 'classify' graduates for the higher civil service. A former ENA graduate, later inspector-general of finance and then Rightist (RPR) senator, Yann Gaillard, noted that ENA functioned like a stable producing race-horses, 'with the one, obsessive idea of preparing for the final examination'. This examination, as he wrote in *Le Monde* (9 March 1997), largely repeated the criteria required for entry into the ENA: predominance of general studies, and priority to oral or written expression at the expense of substance.

A former director of the ENA, Jean Coussirou, also criticized the inability of graduates to overcome the 'dysfunctioning' of the administration that they direct. This failing he attributed to insufficient attention at the ENA to the practical techniques of management of public administration. His successor at ENA, R.-F. Le Bris, agreed that most ENA graduates never experienced the practical work of administration 'in the field': they simply went on to top-level positions, in Paris, equipped with theoretical knowledge. Yet when they did work 'on the job', as in the case of prefects in the provinces, they were much appreciated (R. Rivais in *Le Monde*, 24 April 1997).

The noted sociologist, Michel Crozier, agreed that the training of this 'super-elite' in an 'encyclopaedic and abstract excellence' was not only far removed from training 'on the ground' but also perpetuated the gap between elites and ordinary people. 'French elites, trained to excel but in a very rigid and barely changing mould, are particularly poorly adapted' to the logic of a different world ('A Break on Innovation', *Le Monde de l'éducation*, October 1997).

Similarly Joseph Servan, from the Sorbonne, advocated at least five years of practical experience in public, semi-public or private organizations – in administration, the economy or social work – for those seeking to enter the ENA, but before taking the entrance examination. Such experience, he wrote (*Le Monde*, 3 May 1997), would conform to the practice in other European countries.

Still another critic, Bernard Spitz of the Conseil d'Etat, a graduate of the ENA, attacked the politicians instead. What the public most disliked, he wrote (*Le Monde*, 3 May 1997), is not so much the existence of the ENA, but its former pupils' monopoly of French political life. The public feel that a 'caste' is assured of impunity despite the accumulation of failures, for which they assume neither responsibility nor blame. As for the notorious economic disasters of certain *énarques*: 'Who chose the *énarques* who failed in business? The politicians.'

Instead of selection by talent, as under the Third Republic, Spitz went on, selection of elites now takes place according to 'money, social rank, favouritism'. Suppressing the ENA, therefore, would not solve the problem. For what is needed is to restore an impartial, effective and respected state.

Such, too, was the burden of an important article (*Le Monde*, 15–16 June 1997) by Ezra Suleiman: 'Suppress the ENA or Reform the State?' Real reforms of the public service are required, he insisted. Attacking the ENA is a 'convenient alibi' for politicians, who refuse to face up to the dual task of reforming high public functions and the modernization of the state.

Unlike the situation in Great Britain, and even in Italy, Suleiman continued, France has not even made an effort in this direction. All the governments of the Fifth Republic have acted in a demagogic fashion, as if suppressing the ENA would solve all problems. Instead of correcting the negative tendencies of the ENA – used as a springboard for political or economic careers – politicians have simply advocated 'democratizing' recruitment to the school in a minimal way.

French public figures, Suleiman concludes, refuse to admit that the era of elitism is over. Indeed, France remains the only country where the notion of an all-powerful elite preoccupies political analysis. But in a world characterized by competition and openness, there is little room for an overly self-confident and domineering elite.

How long will France remain an exception to the rule?

References

Berstein, S. (1989) *La France de l'expansion*, vol. 1, Paris: Seuil.

Berstein, S. and Rioux, J.-P. (1995) *La France de l'expansion*, vol. 2, Paris: Seuil.

Birnbaum, P. (1977) *Les Sommets de l'Etat: essai sur l'élite du pouvoir en France*, Paris: Seuil.

Charlot, J. (1994) *La politique en France*, Paris: Fallois.

Julliard, J. (1988) 'La course au centre' in F. Furet, J. Julliard and P. Rosanvallon, *La République du Centre*, Paris: Calmann-Lévy.

Kessler, M.-C. (1978) *ENA: La politique de la haute fonction publique*, Paris: Presses de la FNSP.

——(1994) *Les grands corps de l'Etat*, Paris: PUF.

Mény, Y. (1992) *La corruption de la République*, Paris: Fayard.

Le Monde, various.

Le Monde de l'Education, October 1997.

Le Monde des livres, 4 July 1997.

Stevens, A. (1996) *The Government and Politics of France*, London: Macmillan.

Suleiman, E. (1978) *Elites in French Society*, Princeton, N.J.: Princeton University Press.

——(1995) *Les Ressorts cachés de la réussite française*, Paris: Seuil.

Wright, V. (1989) *The Government and Politics of France*, London: Routledge.

7 Parties

Ce qui me frappait surtout, dans ces partis qui se reformaient, c'était leur désire passionné de s'attribuer en propre, dès qu'ils en auraient l'occasion, tous les pouvoirs de la République et leur incapacité, qu'ils étalaient par avance, de les exercer efficacement.

Charles de Gaulle

Recall the dual nature of the political system (in any liberal-capitalist country): (1) as democratic intermediary between the citizen and the state; and (2) as elitist intermediary between wealth and power. The second aspect, in which politicians defer to the fundamental interests of the economy, requires convergence internally among the major political parties (despite differences of degree) as well as convergence internationally in conformity to European norms and global competition.

If the second aspect is one of convergence, the first aspect (politics as intermediary between citizens and state) is one of specificity: that is, a distinctive approach by one party or another to its electorate. The conservative parties support, in descending order, particular business firms as well as individuals and groups possessing inherited or earned wealth, and then the middle classes, rural interests, etc. Leftist parties support workers and small farmers, the middle classes, city people in general, professionals, mid-level executives and particular business groups.

It is important to note, however, that this first, or democratic, aspect of politics is ultimately subject to the second, elitist, aspect of politics as 'transmission belt' between wealth and power. Politicians, in other words, are perpetually balancing between popular requirements (before and during elections) and economic imperatives, without which the political system could not survive. Currently, as Pierre Rosanvallon points out, the political 'march to the Centre' has profoundly altered the relationship of society to the elites. Rather than the separation of Right and Left, 'Centrism' reveals the separation between elites and masses ('Malaise of

Representation', in Furet, Julliard and Rosanvallon, *La République du Centre*, 142).

To add to the problems of politicians, only the first aspect of politics is considered legitimate, i.e. the relationship between voters and their 'representatives', expressing – in principle – 'democracy of the people, by the people, and for the people', in Lincoln's famous phrase. The second aspect – the relationship between wealth and power – is not considered legitimate, even at the collusive stage: at the 'excessive' stage of corruption it is seen as an obvious abuse of wealth and power.

Politicians therefore emphasize the first, theoretical, aspect of politics and try to conceal, or at least play down, the second, practical, aspect. Hence de Gaulle's strictures (from the quotation above) when the incongruity between the two relationships becomes too great.

One last point: whatever the overriding importance of economics – all the more so in the post-Cold War world – the aspect of democratic legitimacy cannot be ignored: for it is this that gives a sense of purpose, a meaning, to what otherwise is a mere four- or five-year ritual performance. But 'legitimacy' is not an abstraction: it has to be seen in context. And here the economic constraints are such, except during periods of sustained growth, that the results of the ambitious programmes legitimately proposed by politicians almost invariably fall short of the desired objectives.

In the following sections, accordingly, I consider French political parties in terms of this uneasy, dual relationship. First, the basic convergence of Left and Right in regard to the economy – as seen during the 1997 election campaign and after. Second, the issue of leadership, which (if successful) reconciles the two relationships. Leadership, it should be said, is pure politics, going beyond democracy or authoritarianism: it denotes the ability, in a masterly way, to unite tactical skill and strategic objective (de Gaulle is exemplary). Third, party specifics, that is, the relationship between major (and minor) parties and their particular constituents, in both theory and practice. And finally, the opening for reforms, political, administrative and social: notably, judicial independence, the ethical renewal of the state, and social reforms to benefit not the elites but the people.

Economic convergence

The first major demonstration of convergence between Left and Right was the abandonment by the Socialist government in the early 1980s of the planned 'rupture' with capitalism and the adoption instead of policies of economic orthodoxy. The 1997 election campaign – and its consequences

– confirmed the process of convergence. The contest between Left and Right was not over alternative policies but as to which party was best able to 'manage' the economy.

The significance of the 1997 elections was otherwise. It was the resurgence of the Socialists – heavily defeated only four years previously – and the collapse of the conservative coalition, which had expected to win. The result was due not so much to public approval of the appeal of the Left as to its disapproval of the record in government of the Right. This was an outcome that demonstrated both the fluidity and volatility of the electorate – in the absence of clearly marked ideological alternatives – and its capacity to punish a government which had failed to fulfil popular expectations. The problems of the economy – slow growth, a period of recession, and high unemployment – were largely responsible for this failure.

Of all the major issues confronting Right and Left during the 1997 election campaign, most were either directly concerned with the economy or were regarded as an essential component (i.e. as resources) needed to fulfil election promises or commitments. Economic growth – to fund social projects – was central to both Right and Left: the difference between them was one of means – whether to adopt more or less 'neo-liberal' methods (cutting back the role of the state, privatization, reliance on market forces) or Keynesian ideas (boosting domestic demand, maintaining or increasing public expenditure, ensuring job creation, etc.).

Now, the issues debated during the 1997 election campaign *remain* crucial to the success or failure of governments. In the view of the electorate, they are critical to the legitimacy or the discrediting of the democratic parliamentary system. These issues, on which there is a general consensus among Left and Right, can be summarized as follows.

On the central issue of economic management, neither Right nor Left takes up an extreme stance: there is no real support for 'Thatcherite' dogmas, on the one hand, nor statist *dirigisme*, on the other, but rather a fluid consensus on 'social market' capitalism in the middle. After the electoral victory of the Left, the Jospin government confirmed the 'realism' of this consensus.

There is consensus, too, on the need to reduce public expenditure to meet the Maastricht criteria for a single European currency. The Socialists urge certain qualifications, including the need for a social charter, but these are more in the nature of preferences than demands. As for the sceptics on the Right, Philippe Séguin, the major spokesman for 'no' during the 1992 Maastricht referendum, publicly accepts that the issue has been decided. Séguin, after the elimination of his rival, Juppé, had become the 'responsible' head of the neo-Gaullist Right.

Unemployment remains a major challenge to Right and Left. But there is widespread agreement that only sustained economic growth can reduce the unacceptably high rate (over 12 per cent). The Socialists did venture to propose three-quarters of a million new jobs (half in the public sector), but Jospin made plain that this would be over the five-year period of his government. Nevertheless, there is considerable scepticism about the project because of the limited impact of government (any government) on the economy. (On official policies to reduce unemployment, see 'Opening for reform', below.)

Health is another pressing issue for the parties: how to put a stop to the explosion of costs without damaging the scope and quality of health care. The Juppé government had worked out a way to cut inessential costs, which some of the medical associations had accepted but others not. The rejectors were really in favour of unrestricted freedom for them to charge what the market would bear; but their public argument opposed the 'rationing' of health care by funding cuts – as if resources were unlimited! They seemed oblivious to the fact that something had to be done to save the system: if it collapsed, nobody, and especially the sick whose treatment is supposed to be the object of health care, would benefit. The Jospin government, in turn, aimed to reduce the social security deficit considerably by the end of 1998 and achieve a balance in 1999. (See also Chapters 10 and 12 on social security and its implications.)

Insecurity is also near the top of public concern. It is no less a problem for both Right and Left parties – Jospin himself announcing the 'right to security' in October 1997 – partly because of the prominence given to it by Le Pen's National Front, 'stealing' votes from the established parties as a result. Insecurity – crime, drugs, violence in school and in the streets – is a particularly sensitive issue (readily exploited by Le Pen) because of its connection with high unemployment, especially affecting young people (about twice the average rate) and ethnic minorities, of which North Africans are the most numerous. (See especially Chapter 12, 'Identity'.)

Education is hardly less sensitive, given the 'demonstrative' potential of discontented students. It was the student unions that precipitated the wave of public sector strikes in November–December 1995, which did so much to express, and to incite, the alienation of ordinary people from the Juppé government. Yet student dissatisfaction, it is widely agreed, is entirely understandable given the critical state of higher education (though not for the elite): for example, the poor buildings, shortage of teachers, outdated teaching methods (in many cases) and the demoralizing and costly drop-out rate. To attend to all these problems requires massive expenditure, which is just not available. As pointed out in Chapter 3, the one effective way to save money (and thus divert resources to urgent needs) is also not available: because of the 'taboo' on selective entry into the universities.

The independence of the judiciary, proclaimed by Right and Left, is also connected with money, but in a different way. Breaking with the passivity, indulgence or connivance of judges in the past, who simply obeyed orders from the *parquet* (the prosecuting counsel under the minister of justice) to drag out 'sensitive' proceedings or drop them altogether (no case to answer, insufficient evidence), certain judges defied the 'taboo' by investigating cases of corruption and then 'inculpating' suspects. The press supported their efforts by giving publicity to the 'affairs', however embarrassing this might be to political parties or major enterprises which were implicated. Now, because the succession of affairs in the 1980s deeply discredited the Socialists in power and, after their 1993 election disaster, discredited the Right in turn (three ministers in the Balladur government had to resign), both Right and Left came to the conclusion that an image of public integrity required an independent judiciary. President Chirac himself launched the process, while the Jospin government introduced reforms. (See, again, 'Opening for reform', below.)

Even the environment, as long neglected as judicial independence, played a role in the 1997 elections. The Greens, *les Verts*, formed an electoral alliance with the Socialists and won a number of seats; their leader, Dominique Voynet, became environment minister in the Jospin government. While her unhappy predecessor, also an environmentalist, had failed to get the support of the Juppé government to shut down a controversial nuclear reactor, Voynet not only succeeded in this but went on to cancel the equally controversial (and potentially extremely costly) project to link the Rhône and the Rhine by canal! But Voynet was less successful in dealing with pollution, failing to get the support of the 'economic realists' in the Jospin government for heavier duties on (tax-privileged) diesel fuel.

Economic realism

Some months before the 1997 elections, Gilles Martinet, ambassador and former national secretary of the Socialist Party for policy studies, wrote of the need for a new approach by the party, given the seriousness of the economic situation ('The Left in Search of a Programme', *Le Monde*, 11 September 1996). The Centre-Left, he said, is not the same as the Centre-Right (the then Juppé government), but the differences appear quite small. There is no question, unlike the time of the Socialist victory in 1981, of breaking with capitalism and substituting 'nationalization, planning, self-management'. The break instead should be with liberal (market forces) economics, resulting in a different redistribution of the economic surplus, a different organization of labour and the stimulation of economic growth through demand (it is through economic growth that unemployment can be diminished and the hours of work reduced).

Faced with the global economy, the technological revolution and precarious employment, Martinet argued, the Left has lost a good number of its landmarks. Some of its members seek refuge in defence of 'acquired positions' and the rhetoric of political will. One day, the world of nostalgia and illusions will have to be abandoned. Will it be possible before 1998 (the year when elections were intended)?

A year earlier, another national secretary of the Socialist Party, Henri Weber, had proved equally perceptive ('The Three Crises which the Left must Face', *Le Monde*, 8 August 1995). His starting point, too, was the global nature of the economy and the shift in the balance from public to private sector. 'There is no longer a national space, in most European countries, for a grand reformist policy.' The way to the re-establishment of social democracy lies instead in a European context.

The second crisis is the crisis of political representation. It is more and more difficult, Weber went on, for the Socialists to represent simultaneously their two social and electoral bases: the traditional working class and the new salaried middle classes. Economic change has resulted in a growing number of 'excluded', including marginals and the precariously employed, as well as increased taxes on the middle classes (and others) to help the impoverished. The victims of capitalist modernization demand more help and more and better state intervention; the new middle classes resist any increase in their compulsory contributions, needed to fund public policies. The former listen more and more to populist demagogues (read: Le Pen) who propose simple explanations and solutions of their difficulties – and seek scapegoats (foreign migrants, ethnic minorities). Conversely, the middle classes sometimes turn to liberal economics, favouring 'each for himself' and denouncing the abuses of the welfare state. Regaining the popular vote, and especially that of the youth, is the second challenge.

The third crisis is that of party organization and activity. While conditions have changed greatly over twenty years, the party continues to function as it did in 1970, even 1950. The Socialist Party, according to Georges Sarre, has become a 'corporation of elected deputies surrounded by would-be deputies'. This tendency, aggravated by the decline of the Communist Party, leaves the field dangerously open to adventurers.

Jospin's emergence in command of a dispirited, and, to some extent, discredited Socialist Party – 'a field of ruins', in Michel Rocard's famous phrase – followed by his strong show of support in the 1995 presidential campaign against Chirac, certainly energized the party leadership (ending the disastrous infighting of its major 'currents') and mobilized the party activists. But it was public dissatisfaction with the perceived arrogance and ineffectiveness of the Juppé government rather than the renewed popular appeal of the Left that resulted in the downfall of the Right in the 1997 legislative elections. And it was the social problems produced by economic change that played a major part in that dramatic result.

As Jacques Delors, the former head of the European Commission, put it in an interview with *Le Monde* on 17 June 1997:

> Two explanations [for the election results] are possible. The first is that the French remember M. Chirac's promises [during his presidential campaign] and have punished him. The second is that French people are reticent about entering into the twenty-first century and confronting great changes. I cannot yet decide between the two explanations.

Consequently, the Jospin government is on trial, just as the Right was on trial from 1993 to 1997. Economic growth, which is largely beyond government control, is vital to electoral success. But within the limits of what is possible, realistic economic policies – as well as achievable political and social reforms – are essential.

On the one hand, stimulus to economic growth by boosting consumer and salaried demand is considered feasible under conditions of almost nil inflation, successful export drives and the generally healthy state of business – totally unlike the disastrous early 1980s (Laurent Mauduit, *Le Monde*, 4 June 1997). On the other hand, demand-stimulus may raise more problems than it solves. How, in an open and liberal Europe, to avoid capital flight, the drying up of the Paris stock exchange and the inability of business to finance investments, if the government penalizes revenues from shares and other financial placements? How to avoid increased consumer spending on cheaper foreign goods rather than on French products? How to avoid damaging a 'fragile' private sector by the increased weight of the public sector? How to carry out a redistributive and *dirigiste* economic policy and yet claim to adhere to the liberal economic norms of Europe? (P.-L. Séguillon, *La Chaîne Info*, quoted in *Le Monde*, 20 March 1997).

In effect, the Jospin government adhered neither to the Left (dogmatic refusal to continue privatization, insistence on state intervention, large increase in the minimum wage) nor to the Right (reliance on market forces instead) but acted on the consensus of the realists in the major parties, as outlined by Erik Izraelewicz (*Le Monde*, 20 May 1997). 'The Right is not really liberal [economically], the Left is not really Keynesian.' As Jospin himself pointed out, regretting his inability to intervene in Renault's closure of its Belgian subsidiary (noted in Chapter 1): 'We no longer live in an administered economy.'

Among Jospin's first policy decisions was the commitment to respect the Maastricht criteria for a single currency. Moreover, the French and German economic ministers agreed in October 1997 to set up an informal 'Council on the Euro' to coordinate policies. Jospin himself publicly endorsed access to the Internet – the first time French political leaders clearly favoured the worldwide 'information highway' over the now outmoded domestic Minitel. (In mid-1997, only 28 per cent of French businesspeople were connected to the Internet in their homes, compared with 36 per cent in Britain and 48 per cent in Germany.)

And even if the word 'privatization' was not invoked by the Jospin government, 'adaptation' to the market was. A number of the remaining nationalized firms, including France Télécom, were listed for an infusion of private capital (leaving the state as an important or major shareholder) or outright privatization, following the policy of the Juppé government. This is a pragmatic policy, commentators point out, deciding issues case by case – a policy, moreover, that is in line with the 'logic of industry', since the government is unable to provide the funds needed for industrial restructuring, while the revenue obtained from privatization is a windfall which can be used for other purposes.

Also intended to remedy a major defect of the French 'exception' – capitalism without capital, it is said – is the favourable attitude of Jospin and Economic Minister Strauss-Kahn (despite earlier reservations) towards private pension funds, as developed in Britain and America.

Leadership

Jospin's 'realism of the Left', aimed at producing a broad consensus on policies within and outside government, clearly expresses his leadership strategy. As Charlot points out, in the France of the Fifth Republic, leadership plays the crucial role of 'presidentializing' the major political parties. The Constitution requires a leader; the major parties have to produce one if their candidate as president is to be credible. Leadership, as noted above, is pure politics, going beyond democratic or parliamentary regimes: it is the ability, in a masterly way, to unite tactical skills with strategic objectives. De Gaulle, founder of the Fifth Republic, is exemplary. 'Take responsibility for action,' as he wrote in his *Mémoires de guerre – L'Appel*, 'and confront destiny alone': such are the characteristics of the leader.

Even during the years of opposition, between the postwar provisional government of France and the fall of the Fourth Republic, de Gaulle toured the country, consulted, held meetings meticulously organized by

Malraux and Soustelle, and galvanized his forces. The action of his 'rassemblement' of the French people was national, not partisan, in his eyes. His struggle was to free the state from the dictatorship of the parties, not to win seats or form coalitions. The virtues of 'assembling' the people allowed him to give priority to creating new forms of democracy, by consultation, association and mobilization of the citizens. Whatever his opponents said (and the Communists insisted that he was a 'fascist') de Gaulle's movement was in the historic tradition of Bonapartism, largely transcending the cleavage between Left and Right. The annual national sessions of the movement were more like a religious mass – an invitation to action by the whole people – rather than a machine for fabricating motions and majorities (Rioux, 218).

When in power, in the early 1960s, de Gaulle's movement rejected an ideological stance, presenting itself instead as a party of modern management turned towards the emerging and dynamic categories of the population: executives, doctors, engineers, technicians. The party apparatus was centralized, ruled in an authoritarian fashion, for its purpose was to transmit to the country the orders issued from the Elysée (the presidency) which were carried out by the government (Berstein, 95, also 127).

Georges Pompidou, closely associated with de Gaulle and for six years his prime minister, undoubtedly adhered as president to the same conception of the grandeur of France and the power of the state. But, from his career as a banker, he was aware of the economic realities of the modern world: that it was impossible to have a powerful state and a great nation without economic prosperity – of which industrialization, in a world dominated by market forces and liberal economic values, was the key. Pompidou as president showed his deep attachment to these values, emphasizing entrepreneurship and the profit motive, which led him to favour industrial concentration and the formation of large enterprises – a policy far removed from his country heritage of (Third Republic) radicalism in defence of the 'small man' (Berstein and Rioux, 28–30).

Jacques Chirac, founder of the present Rassemblement pour la République, inherited these two strands of Gaullism: the paternalistic social-reformism of de Gaulle, and the technocratic drive for profit and efficiency. From his base as mayor of Paris (from 1977 to the eve of his successful presidential campaign in 1995) and as unassailable head of the Gaullist Party, Chirac strengthened his bid to displace Giscard d'Estaing (former president, but defeated by Mitterrand in 1981) as effective leader of the Right. 'With his optimism, his dynamism and immense energy, his capacity to elicit great loyalty, his series of clientalistic networks', Chirac became prime minister ('cohabiting' with Mitterrand) in 1986–8 and president in 1995 (Wright, 195–6).

Giscard, whose efforts to establish a dominant Centre-Right grouping, rivalling the Gaullists, foundered after his presidential term came to an end, set out to provide an alternative model for the Right, defined as 'liberal, Centrist and European'. This formula was intended to distinguish his 'federation' of parties from the Gaullists, implicitly characterized as '*dirigiste*, rightist and nationalist' (Berstein, 132). Giscard, elected as president (with the support of Chirac) following the death of Pompidou in 1974, presented himself as a modern, reformist leader, appealing to the administrative and economic elite. His first years as president were indeed marked by valuable social reforms – sale of contraceptives permitted, divorce by mutual consent, legislation on abortion – but Giscard's 'government from the centre' was increasingly blocked by Gaullist resistance and the inability of the regime to overcome major economic problems (the end of *les Trente Glorieuses*). Defeated by Mitterrand in 1981, Giscard's own leadership of the Union pour la démocratie française was enfeebled. Indeed, the UDF suffers from a double tension, as Charlot points out (p. 99): internally, between its two main constituents – the Parti républicain, which for a long time was dominant, and the Centre des démocrates sociaux, which aimed to dominate; and externally with the 'ally-rival', the Gaullist RPR.

François Mitterrand performed an even more difficult 'rassemblement' of the Left. (A good critical summary is by Serge Berstein, 'Les deux septennats de François Mitterrand', 1996.) Combining great ambition, organizing talents and unrivalled experience of the parliamentary scene, he brought together in 1971 the disparate and dejected groups and parties of the Left to found a new Socialist Party which, allied strategically with the Communists, swept to power in 1981. Whatever the disillusionment caused by his second term as president – economic crises, corruption scandals, palace intrigues, cynical manipulation replacing the former inspiration – Mitterrand's earlier achievement was basic to Jospin's own leadership of a reinvigorated party and its success in the 1997 elections.

Party characteristics

Gaullist ideas and attitudes still exert a major influence on the Right. The RPR is more disciplined and coherent than the fragmented UDF; it is mass-based in contrast to the elitist UDF; and it is strongly implanted locally with about one-fifth of the mayors of cities (of over 9,000 inhabitants), a quarter of general councillors and a third of presidents of regions (Charlot, 90).

Nevertheless, there are discordant strands, varying from the social-Gaullism of Philippe Séguin (displacing the defeated Alain Juppé as head of the RPR in 1997: a potential contender for the presidency) to the populist-Rightism of Charles Pasqua (law and order, controls on immigration) and the modified economic liberalism of Edouard Balladur (prime minister after 1993 and rival of Chirac for the presidency in 1995), each with their loyal following. (See S. Hazareesingh on the erosion of Gaullist hegemony over the Right; and the basic cleavage as to whether the RPR should be a 'party of order' or a 'party of movement': *Political Traditions in Modern France*, 279–81.)

As for the 'spirit' of Gaullism, it is passionately invoked by a writer close to Chirac, Denis Tillinac, who is no less critical of the arrogant, technocratic, elitist strand identified with the unfortunate Juppé. Gaullism, on the contrary, is

> plebeian, sentimental, on the moving frontiers of Bonapartism, populism and anarchism . . . .A Gaullist loves insubordination (like the General in regard to Vichy), despises notables and burns to draw his sword . . . to fight socialites, the powerful, those who fear danger and the rich.
>
> (Tillinac's outpouring of grief at the Rightist defeat in 1997, *Le Monde*, 4 June 1997)

Another, less sympathetic, side of the RPR has been revealed with its overtures, if not to Le Pen himself, at least to voters of the National Front. (More of these voters, in the second round of the 1997 elections, supported the Left than the Right.) In a transparent attempt to regain their support, the RPR senator Alain Peyrefitte asserted the common values shared by the Right and the extreme-Right: patriotism; priority given to the 'superior interests of the country'; safeguarding national identity; Europe (but respecting the character of the states composing it); 'the spirit of defence and an army guaranteeing security'; an independent foreign policy; 'strict protection of the victims of insecurity and firmness in the fight against criminals, delinquency and terrorism'; control of immigration; protection of the family.

In ceasing to defend these 'fundamental values' and leaving them to be taken over by the extreme-Right, argued the senator, the Right was 'rejecting an important part of its electorate' (article in *Le Monde*, 17 June 1997). Juppé and Séguin, to their credit, refused any agreement with the National Front. The issue became critical following the March 1998 local elections – especially for the UDF – when five regional leaders, including Charles Millon, accepted National Front votes to retain their posts. They were then expelled from their parties. Chirac, in turn, denounced any compromise with the 'racist' National Front, which was contrary to Republican values.

As for the reconstruction of the UDF, following the 1997 election defeat, which halved its parliamentary strength, its president, François Léotard, a Balladur supporter, sought to reunify his 'liberal and centrist family'. Alain Madelin, the devotee of market forces (stern opponent of state intervention and hierarchical decisions), took over as head of the once larger component of the UDF, the Parti républicain, later re-named Démocratie libérale, only to split from the UDF in May 1998. Meanwhile François Bayrou, who supported Chirac as president (and became minister of education), was made leader of the now bigger component, Force démocrate (previously CDS), and head of the UDF deputies in the assembly. After the shock of the 1997 election defeat, nearly three-quarters of RPR supporters and two-thirds of UDF supporters advocated the fusion of the two groupings (*Le Figaro*, 29 August 1997); but leaders were unwilling to give up control of their own particular groups. To avert a crisis, Léotard and Séguin, leader of the disintegrating UDF and hardly less divided RPR, decided in May 1998 to join a confederal 'Alliance' opposed to the Left and the extreme-Right. Yet the alienation of citizens from factional politicians, who put ambitions before principles, is evident from *La Figaro's* survey of 25 May 1998.

As for the Left, united in victory (Communists, Socialists, Greens and others participated in the Jospin government), the most striking historical change has been the reversal of fortunes of Communists and Socialists. The Communist Party, inheritor of a fine resistance record and staunch 'voice of the people', was by far the biggest vote-winner in postwar France. But by the Gaullist era of the 1960s, the Communists – led by doctrinaire Stalinists, incapable of adapting to change, facing the erosion of their industrial base – were in irreversible decline. In the 1970s they were surpassed, for the first time, by the Socialists. In 1997, despite a new reformist leader, Robert Hue, their vote was less than one million compared to nearly ten million for the Socialists. (The 'implosion' of the Communist Party is dramatically depicted by Hazareesingh: 300–11; see also his incisive survey of Socialism: 231–58.)

The Greens, thanks to the electoral alliance struck by their leader Dominique Voynet with the Socialists, won seven seats in the 1997 national assembly (and nearly a million votes in the *first* round of elections). Voynet has made an impact with her decisions to close down the controversial Superphénix nuclear reactor and cancel the massive Rhine–Rhône canal project. She may thus have vindicated her 'pragmatic' approach to politics, replacing the 'ideological' stance of non-political purity advocated by the first important leader of the Greens, Antoine Waechter. The latter was evicted after bitter infighting, unhappily characteristic of the sectarianism (aggravated by personal rivalry) of many minor movements.

Personal rivalries may also mark the downfall of the National Front
once its charismatic but unscrupulous leader, Le Pen, leaves the scene.
Until now the Front's spectacular advance (to some 15 per cent of the vote
for Le Pen at the 1988 presidential elections) and the control of the important city of Toulon as well as some other municipalities in the South has
amazed – and shocked – public opinion. (Some three-quarters of those
polled early in 1997 considered the Front to be a danger to democracy as
well as racist.) In the first round of the 1997 elections, the Front polled
3,750,000 votes – more than 1,000,000 higher than the Communists. In
the March 1998 local elections, the Front, with over 15 per cent of total
votes, played a pivotal role, undermining in particular the 'moderate'
Right. Nowhere in Europe, apart from Austria, has the extreme-Right
shown such strength.

How can one account for this disturbing phenomenon? One answer is
that Le Pen, too, has displayed unusual qualities of leadership by attracting
and dominating by force of personality many disparate elements of French
society. At one period, the Front had more support from the working class
than the Communist Party: the Front is also a party of protest against insecurity in the towns and suburbs, against massive unemployment, against a
supranational Europe and, above all, against the 'corrupt', ineffectual and
elitist politicians. According to a survey in June 1997, around a quarter of
the working class, the unemployed and those with only primary education
support the National Front; thus, it attracts the socially and culturally
deprived, those most affected by the economic crisis and those who fear for
the future (*Le Monde*, 5 June 1997).

Second, Le Pen attracts the 'deep Right' of France, such as traditionalist Catholics, despairing at the impact of a 'permissive society', the loss of
family values, the rise in the divorce rate, the growth of single-parent
households, and so on. Third, Le Pen deliberately says aloud (for the
publicity value of provocation) what a substantial number of French
people keep to themselves: dislike of Arab and African immigrants, suspicion of their involvement in drugs and crime, anger at their supposed
displacement of French workers (in fact the immigrants do the menial jobs
that French people prefer not to do), irritation at the social services
'foreigners' unduly acquire, fear of being swamped by 'others' in their own
country, fear of change in their society – in a word, racism. (See Chapter
12, 'Identity'.)

So long as '*morosité*' (despondency, gloom) is so prevalent in France, so
long as the economy fails to make progress, so long as the country feels the
stress of global competition and European constraints, then the National
Front is likely to endure, if not advance. But it is possible, as some of its
younger leaders envisage, that once the commanding figure of Le Pen is

absent from the scene, then the Front might evolve (like the Italian neo-Fascists) into an 'acceptable' party of the Right.

Opening for reform

The economic situation, in its positive and its negative aspects, exerts a remarkable impact on all the political parties, big or small. Nevertheless, despite economic uncertainties and the pressure of international competition, there is an opening for reform – in the administration, politics and society – for governments of the Left, as in France and Italy, and the Centre-Left, as in Tony Blair's Britain. The situation is more complicated for Clinton's Centrist regime, despite its economic advantages – sustained growth, low unemployment compared with Europe, and relatively low inflation – because of the Republican control of Congress and the swing in public opinion against 'big government'.

Reform of justice

Reforms are not only possible but necessary in the present state of French society. Such is the burden of the appeal, launched on 11 May 1997, by more than a hundred members of the judiciary, including sixteen from the Court of Appeal (*Cour de cassation*) and thirty from lower appeal courts. About one-third of signatories were from the Leftist Syndicat de la magistrature, another third (according to *Le Monde*) are considered either Centrist – such as the majority Union syndicale des magistrats – or from the Right.

The main thrust of the appeal was for the guaranteed independence of the judiciary (from political pressure), precisely because of the prevalence of 'affairs' which not only jeopardize the basic rules of law – the essential principles of the Republic – but because the apparent immunity of important figures outrages the sense of justice and the respect for equality of all citizens before the law.

The appeal noted in evidence:

> Theft of documents confided to public authorities, illegal wiretapping, transfer of funds by political parties to safe-havens [*paradis fiscaux*], refusal of elected deputies and police officials to submit to judicial procedures, corruption indulged in by enterprises in France or in foreign markets, diversion of funds received from the public . . . the picture is grim.

The 'Republican pact', the signatories went on, is the first victim of this degradation of public life. The mission of the judges is to apply the law and to guarantee the individual freedoms of all. Therefore 'they should not submit to *raison d'Etat*, nor to global economic interests'. But the judges alone cannot redeem democracy or uphold Republican values:

> Democracy is not a space that is void of political, civic or ethical rules. It is a practice, a spirit, which should also inspire the functioning of institutions as well as individual behaviour, especially those with public or private responsibilities. It is founded on the search for the common good.

A further appeal was launched by the '103' (with many more supporters) to President Chirac, Prime Minister Jospin and Justice Minister Elisabeth Guigou in July 1997. It emphasized that the impartiality of French justice, guaranteed by its independence, was more than ever imperative. 'Often promised, never assured, [judicial independence] is the key to the true progress of democracy.' Otherwise, who is to assure the legitimacy of public activity? What can guarantee that the formula 'justice is rendered in the name of the French people' corresponds to reality? How is the work of judges to be judged? (Note Hazareesingh's scepticism, referring to a 'weak and demoralized judiciary, which has been constantly vulnerable to external political pressures': *Political Traditions in Modern France*, 170–1.)

The Truche Commission on the reform of justice, appointed by President Chirac, did recommend in July 1997 that the prosecution (*parquet*) – under the authority of the minister of justice – should not interfere in individual cases being examined by the investigating judges; but it did not propose the independence of the judiciary. Instead, the existing division between prosecution (under ministerial authority) and investigation should continue. *Le Monde* on 12 July 1997 helpfully recorded 'Six Years of Hesitations and Political Reversals under the Pressure of Affairs', noting the way in which the Socialist government removed the 'sensitive' Urba dossier of political corruption from the investigating judge in 1991, how the moderate union of magistrates had recommended that the *parquet* should be protected from 'political power' in 1992 followed by the 'somersaults' of Justice Minister Toubon in the Chirac–Juppé government – boldly proclaiming non-intervention in 'affairs' to start with and then reverting to the usual practice of withholding evidence, delaying procedures and not initiating prosecution.

The Jospin government clearly espoused the principle of judicial independence: Jospin 'solemnly announced' on 19 June 1997 that there would be no government interference. The minister of justice then proposed a 'profound reform' in October 1997 to assure the independence of the judiciary.

At the same time, however, the distinguished constitutional lawyer, Robert Badinter, warned that so long as appointments and promotions were in the hands of the ministry, the judges would still be dependent on their political masters. Another objection of a different sort was raised by Philippe Séguin, who asserted in March 1997 that 'our democratic principles' would not permit the equal status of an independent judiciary with that of the elected representatives of the people.

Yet another constitutional issue was Jospin's preference for a five-year (and not seven-year) presidential term: an important issue during a period of cohabitation. The Jospin government also moved to 'de-dramatize' the controversial problem of immigration, following the report of an independent expert, Patrick Weil, in July 1997. The report emphasized that states have the right to control the entry of foreigners, but in the context of 'superior rules': refusal of ethnic selection, the right to asylum and to family life, and the right of residents to integration. The Jospin government presented its proposed law in October 1997 – a law which did not satisfy some on the Left and many on the Right.

Accumulation of mandates

The Socialist government moved into another controversial area: the question of the *cumul des mandats*. Reformers have long denounced this unusual practice: another 'French exception' to the rule of the rest of Europe. But while a parliamentary 'working group' headed by the Social-Gaullist Philippe Séguin in 1994 agreed that the system was conducive to 'conflicts of interest' when legislators were also executives (responsible for public works contracts), its members were divided over banning the *cumul* – and so 'no decision could be reached'. Jospin in his 19 June 1997 policy statement, however, promised to bring in legislation to limit the accumulation.

Admittedly, the Westminster parliamentary system also 'accumulates' legislative and executive powers – but this is at the national level. There is a great difference between an elected parliamentary majority deciding on general issues of policy (including local government) and one whose deputies are simultaneously local executives, as mayors of cities or towns (perhaps also as members of departmental or regional councils). As for the argument often advanced in France that a highly centralized country requires nationally elected politicians to have effective local connections, this can surely be achieved (as in Britain and elsewhere) by regular attendance to their constituencies – without adopting a 'cumulative' system that is conducive to manipulation.

Employment

Seventy per cent of those polled at the time of the May–June 1997 elections gave priority to job creation (the Socialists planned to create 700,000 new jobs, half in the public sector, over a five-year period); 55 per cent wanted an increase in the minimum wage (SMIC; Jospin did raise it by 4 per cent, considered a 'moderate' increase by commentators and 'realistic' by the government); 35 per cent sought political reforms, including a ban on the *cumul*, as pledged by Jospin. But reducing the hours of work – another Socialist pledge – seemed much less urgent to those polled (see below).

Martine Aubry's project to create 350,000 jobs for young people was an innovative – but so far untested – attempt both to provide work and to meet social needs, such as help for dependent people, prevention of violence, co-ordinating school support and offering family mediation (see the list of job proposals in *Le Monde*, 21 August 1997).

The dilemma of all the advanced countries, however, as former US Secretary of Labor Robert Reich explains, is whether to choose the American model of high employment with substantial part-time work, low wages and precarious prospects, or the European model of severe unemployment mitigated by extensive welfare services. Reich himself, writing for the *Guardian* of 14 July 1997, urges a third way. Maximum flexibility for employers he considers essential if they are to create more jobs; and they must be able to dismiss unneeded or poorly performing workers. Conversely, fairness requires a minimum wage, along with health and pension benefits. Workplace adaptability and welfare reforms – to provide incentives for those on welfare to go to work – come second. And third are policies facilitating economic growth. These reforms are hard to implement, Reich concedes. Hence the challenge of leadership: 'persuading all parties to make a deal'.

'Flexibility', however, is a bad word to French Socialists – not to speak of the trade unions – and 'dismissal of the unneeded' is equally unacceptable. To the employers, on the other hand, economic growth cannot be achieved without a flexible labour market and unhindered retrenchment of the work force if needed. Given the French tradition of intransigent boss–labour relations, the consensus approach favoured by the Jospin government (and successfully carried out in the Netherlands in the sense of Reich's recommendations) failed in its first major test: the obligatory imposition of a thirty-five-hour week by the year 2000.

For the Socialists, the shorter hours of work would create more jobs; for the *patrons*, to the contrary, it would simply add to the costs of production. Jospin, moreover, felt obliged, for the sake of political credibility, to uphold his election promise (in contrast to the behaviour of Chirac). The employers, for the sake of economic credibility, equally felt obliged to refuse the imposition of the thirty-five-hour week by a majority of politicians, rather than by negotiation among the 'social partners'.

The Socialists will be judged, then, on two fundamental issues: their ability to reduce unemployment and their ability to reinvigorate political life. The latter requires, above all, an effective campaign against corruption and thus an end to political interference with the course of justice. Only in this way will the integrity of public life and the legitimacy of politics be restored in the eyes of French citizens.

References

Berstein, S. (1989) *La France de l'expansion*, vol. 1, Paris: Seuil.

——(1996) 'Les deux septennats de François Mitterrand', *Modern and Contemporary France*, vol. NS4, no. 1.

Berstein, S. and Rioux, J.-P. (1995) *La France de l'expansion*, vol. 2, Paris: Seuil.

Charlot, J. (1994) *La politique en France*, Paris: Fallois.

Le Figaro, 27 August 1997.

Gaulle, Ch. de (1954) *Mémoires de guerre – L'Appel 1940–1942*, Paris: Plon.

Guardian, 14 July 1997.

Hazareesingh, S. (1994) *Political Traditions in Modern France*, Oxford: Oxford University Press.

Rioux, J.-P. (1980) *La France de la Quatrième République*, vol. 1, Paris: Seuil.

Rosanvallon, P. (1988) 'Malaise dans la représentation' in F. Furet, J. Julliard and P. Rosanvallon, *La République du Centre*, Paris: Calmann-Lévy.

Wright, V. (1989) *The Government and Politics of France*, London: Routledge.

8 Affairs

La collaboration d'une partie des milieux d'affaires ... l'étalage du
mercantilisme, le contraste entre la pénurie ... et le luxe de quelques-uns,
exaspéraient la masse française.

Charles de Gaulle

The tendency to corruption – the scandal of repeated 'affairs' – is
common to all countries. What is specific to a given country, such as
France, is the particular form (or forms) that corruption takes. Thus,
corruption anywhere cannot be understood – let alone corrected – without
understanding the 'structural' conditions that make corruption possible. In
this chapter, accordingly, I first analyse the structural or general conditions
of corruption before considering French 'specificity' – that is, forms pecu-
liar to France.

Corruption is always present. For corruption, evident in past centuries,
does not disappear as countries develop and modernize. Instead, it takes
on new forms. Corruption basically derives from the 'mismatch' between
the new force of capitalism – dominant since the end of the Cold War –
and the old force of democracy, which was born in a different age and
under very different, and more egalitarian, social and economic conditions. The situation today is entirely changed: enormous economic
interests now weigh on political decisions. Thus, corruption today is symptomatic of a deeper problem: the collusive system in which politicians
mediate the often contradictory claims of capitalism and democracy.

To recall: the intermediary role of political parties is crucial. It operates
along two dimensions. The first, avowed, mediation is between the citizen
and the state, which in accordance with democratic theory imparts legitimacy to the system. The second, unavowed, mediation is between business
interests and political decisions, acting in effect as a transmission belt
between wealth and power.

The tendency to corruption, in the 'advanced' and 'undeveloped' countries alike, derives from this second, intermediary, role. For even in the advanced countries the practice of democracy – as distinct from its 'pure' theory – gives priority to business interests rather than to citizens' demands. To act otherwise is to risk economic collapse and, with it, political and social chaos. The resulting 'collusion' between politicians and business is the normal state of affairs. It is when collusion develops to excess, leading to the abuse of public office for private gain, that corruption appears.

To summarize:

1 corruption is a structural condition – the 'excessive' expansion of capitalism, penetrating non-economic (political and social) spheres; such penetration is the effect, directly, of the pressure of capitalist interests on public policy decisions and, indirectly, of the pervasive influence of commercialized values on consumers/electors;

2 this situation of economic penetration is normatively defined: taken to excess, corruption represents the perversion of principles (such as the 'good society') upon which a political system is founded;

3 normative definition expresses the conflict, in important respects, between capitalism and democracy, for each has absolute claims on society (against each other). The very notion of 'popular sovereignty' is one of 'full power' to control all aspects of society, including the economic; capitalism, in turn, implicates all citizens in their work, how they make a living, indeed their way of life;

4 confronting these claims, even politicians of integrity have to compromise between the interests of the public and the interests of business;

5 if and when the norms of public integrity lose their force, then politicians, accustomed to the habitual compromises of economic-political relations, 'drift' into corruption.

In this chapter, accordingly, I emphasize the underlying causes of corruption: the clash between the imperatives of capitalism and the claims of 'popular sovereignty' expressed by democracy. Then I consider, in turn, modern inducements to corruption, notably commercialization of values and electoral funding; then the 'specificities' of French practice, including the *cumul des mandats* and the conflicts of interest arising out of decentralization; and finally the danger to democracy posed by corruption. (See John Girling, *Corruption, Capitalism and Democracy*, Preface, Introduction, Conclusion.)

Underlying causes

Corruption stems from the ambiguous relations between capitalism and democracy: each, in principle, has overriding claims over the other. But, in practice, it is capitalism that structures society, dictating how people work and what they have to live on, according to the assets they have (or do not have) to exchange in the 'free market'.

Democracy, in principle, expresses the sovereignty of the 'people's will': in Lincoln's famous phrase, 'government of the people, by the people, and for the people'. In practice, the democratic political system also structures society – but indirectly and intermittently. As a result, political equality is contrasted with economic inequality. It is the inequality of economic assets in society combined with the requirement of any political system to sustain itself materially that forms the basis for capitalist penetration of other, ostensibly non-economic, spheres.

Now, the ambiguity of economic–political relations is revealed, on the one hand, in the evident correlation between economic freedom (market exchange) and political freedom (liberal democracy) and, on the other hand, in the contrast between capitalist values (private appropriation, profit-motive) and social values (popular sovereignty, the 'public good').

Paradoxically, where capitalism is most compatible with democracy – through the improvement of material living standards so that electoral choices are no longer constrained by poverty – it is precisely in this way that capitalism (consumerism, commercialized values) penetrates non-economic spheres, contrary to democratic theorizing. Indeed, the very hallmark of 'modernity', the distinction between public and private concerns which is basic to legal-rational politics and administration, is conflated in capitalist practice.

Now, it is because of the public/private distinction that politicians, in a democracy, are considered to be 'people's representatives' and bureaucrats are 'public servants'. They are concerned, in principle, not with advancing their private interests but only with what is conducive to the public good.

The raison d'être of capitalism, to the contrary, is private profit, derived from the operation of a competitive market. Market values guide behaviour. Thus, buying voters, legislators and state officials is 'good business' if it produces cost-effective results. Obviously such practice, from the normative standpoint of democracy, is a deformation of the principle of 'government by the people'. Yet, realistically, the economic system has an undeniable impact on the political, which in democratic theory it should not have. It should be the other way round.

One way to bridge the gap between theory and practice is to establish either legal or at least 'acceptable' or informal channels of influence between wealth and power. (This is what I have called 'collusion'.) Corruption is another way.

The logic of collusion is to accommodate politics to economics, that is, to serve the interests of capitalism: this is known as 'economic development'. 'Thatcherism' – the 'neo-liberal' economics dominant in Britain and the United States and challenging the 'social market' in the rest of Europe – realizes this logic instinctively. That is why 'society' – a political expression – did not exist for Thatcher. Instead of society there is only, at least fundamentally, the relationship between producers and consumers, mediated by the market.

Yet if democracy is to have any meaning for people it must lie in the reassertion of non-economic ideals and interests – even against those of the market. This means the assertion of democracy's authentic values: political freedom, popular consent, sovereignty. Conversely, as attested by the Nolan Committee on standards in public life in Britain, and by Jospin and Séguin emphasizing the ethical role of the state in France, it is precisely the weakening of public values (partly as a result of 'neo-liberal' attacks) that undermines the barriers to corruption.

Corruption, to repeat, is the practice of collusion taken to excess: 'the unacceptable face of capitalism', as another British prime minister (Edward Heath) once put it. Corruption, by 'going too far', *exposes* what is normally hidden from view: the collusive system of elites furthering the expansion of capitalist practice and market values at the expense of demo-cratic practice and public values. This is a general problem; but it is also a particular problem for France.

Modern inducements

Commercialization of values, electoral funding by business firms and the potent influence of lobbying clearly illustrate capitalist penetration into non-economic spheres – political and social – in advanced and developing countries alike.

Commercialization of values is evident from Weber's magisterial account of *The Protestant Ethic and the Spirit of Capitalism*. The Protestant ethic, as Weber points out, had to overcome traditional ways of thinking (such as the earlier religious condemnation of usury) before the capitalist spirit could emerge, by way of devotion to the 'calling' of making money. The 'this-worldly asceticism' of the Puritans, both in Britain and in America, favoured not merely the accumulation of capital, but a 'rational bourgeois economic life' of hard work, thrift, calculation, self-control and methodical organization (Weber, 174).

'By the proper use of wealth,' advised D.S. Gregory, author of a text-book on Christian ethics widely used in late nineteenth-century America, 'man may greatly elevate and extend his moral work . . . .It is his duty to secure wealth for this high end' (quoted by Gail Kennedy, ed., *Democracy and the Gospel of Wealth*, 59). From religion to politics is a short step. Thus,

Alexander Hamilton, 'realist' statesman during and after the period of American independence: 'Money is, with propriety, considered as the vital principle of the body politic' (*The Federalist Papers*, no. 30).

Similarly, in present-day France, the 'affairs' of the 1980s and 1990s reveal both subtle and systematic linkages between economic and political power holders. As Yves Mény explains in his authoritative work *La corruption de la République*, influence-peddling, 'sale' of decisions, abuse of public functions, commissions from deals, and misappropriation of public funds are all forms of current behaviour. But they are characterized by 'complicity' and 'arrangement', rather than direct monetary exchange, thus blurring the distinction between the legal and the illicit, between morality and immorality. As a result, public authority is increasingly being transformed into a 'market actor': products (decisions) are exchanged for political or economic 'returns', which sometimes are of advantage to the community and sometimes benefit particular individuals (Mény, 13–17).

The Rozès Commission on corruption (appointed by Prime Minister Balladur) confirmed in December 1994 that 'the most serious and frequent situations' are not so much 'buying' a market or a definite public decision but rather 'the interweaving in the course of time of close and often ambiguous relations between political and economic decision-makers'. Rozès concludes:

> We have lived in a period of exceptional economic expansion, during which many believed that anything was possible. Then, in the recent recession, certain people tried to hold on to their gains . . . .Little by little, the notion of a great public service has crumbled away. When one sees that certain things happen without being punished, one develops the habit . . . [and] morality itself is eroded.

Electoral funding, too, reveals throughout the world the influence of business on politics. The scandal of the unauthorized financing of Clinton's successful presidential campaign in 1996, for example, is notorious. Even in Britain, long reputed for the probity of its public life, the Conservative Party (in power from the 1980s to the mid-1990s) persistently refused to investigate, let alone prohibit, dubious sources of external business finance.

The Socialist Party in France, also in power during the 1980s and early 1990s (until the disastrous election defeat in 1993), was even more tainted by electoral-financing scandals. One major reason for their discredit was the contrast between their leaders' high moral stance before assuming power – 'What we must dislodge is monopoly,' declaimed François Mitterrand in 1971, 'indeed, all the powers of money, money which kills, which buys, which destroys, and which corrupts even the conscience of men' – and the way in which their 'conscience' was so easily, if subtly, corrupted once in power. (The way was to receive secret commissions from favoured businesses granted public works and other contracts, which were laundered through so-called 'planning bureaux' and then used to finance electoral campaigns: admittedly, the Socialists were short of money, which was hardly the case with their Right-wing opponents.) The opportunistic 'amnesty' provided to deputies involved in such practices – once these schemes had been revealed – did not endear the Socialists to their electors.

When the Right came to power it had at least learned this lesson. (This is not to say that corruption has come to an end: far from it!) The Rozès Commission specifically recommended the prohibition of all business funding of political activities. Such funding, it argued, even when carried out openly, 'gives rise to suspicion as to an eventual return of favours'. 'Enterprises do not provide gifts,' as the National Assembly's working group on corruption put it, 'without expecting something in return, in one form or another.' The Balladur government voted to prohibit such funding in January 1995; and the provisions for public funding of candidates were reinforced. (See also Girling, 106–13.)

Conflicts of interest: *cumuls* and decentralization

Is French 'exceptionalism' also to blame for conditions of corruption that are more prevalent than in most other countries in Western Europe? The answer is 'yes', in the sense that the 'accumulation of mandates' by elected representatives – national and local members, combining legislative and executive functions – is a French phenomenon virtually unknown elsewhere; and that such an accumulation of powers, ensuring conflicts of interest, is intimately linked with the tendency to corruption. Indeed, local government throughout the world is more susceptible to corrupt deals (with builders and developers, with transport firms and with supermarkets) than is national government. Thus, when the two are combined, as the practice of *cumuls* and decentralization are combined, then it is not surprising that corruption becomes an 'everyday affair'.

Such is the conclusion, in effect, of the National Assembly's working group on corruption, headed by Philippe Séguin. As the report of the group observed (in November 1994),

> the accumulation of mandates and elective functions favours . . .
> conflicts of interest, which can provoke suspicion, if not leading to
> reprehensible conduct. Even if parliamentarians as such are not
> subject to solicitation by powerful industrial and financial groups, they

cannot avoid making contact with them when they are at the same time managers of local collectivities.

The working group calculated that of the 577 deputies in 1994, 89 were also regional councillors, 248 were (departmental) general councillors, 20 were councillors in Paris, 83 were mayors of towns or cities of 20,000 inhabitants or more, 6 were deputy-mayors of cities of over 100,000, and 4 were deputies to the European Parliament. Yet, despite the inherent conflicts of interest in the practice of *cumuls*, 'certain members of the [working] group' could not bring themselves to forbid it. It was left to Prime Minister Jospin, following the 1997 elections, to commit himself to ending the French exception.

The Assembly's working group also criticized the abuses of decentralization: that is, the delegation of executive functions to local and regional collectivities, inaugurated by the Socialists in the 1980s. As the report delicately put it,

> It is necessary to state that the practice of public works contracts and the delegation of public services may lend themselves, despite the efforts of the legislator, to all sorts of practices, reported in recent judicial cases, including false billing, secret financial transactions, malversation, corruption.

Mény's own assessment emphasizes that the 'absence of countervailing powers and controls' and the existence of 'parallel structures' of authority have contributed largely to such 'deviations'. It is not the honesty of most elected representatives that is at stake, he writes, but rather the

> system of power and management founded on the almost exclusive authority of one person – the 'accumulating' notable – as the central element of a network in which effectiveness replaces legality, where clientalism is substituted for the state of law, and where the separation of public and private spheres is blurred by the confusion of the two.
>
> (Mény, 95; see also *Projet*, no. 232, 'Attention Corruption!')

Danger to democracy

'Public corruption', reported the Rozès Commission, 'has the most serious consequences' because it alters the link between government and governed, elected and electors; 'it unravels the social contract and de-symbolizes politics, which is then reduced to an association of interests where everything is negotiated, bought and sold.' It is this elitist 'association of interests' – from the local 'notable' to the high official, divorced from the needs of ordinary people – which leads in particular cases to corruption, and as a general consequence to the 'democratic deficit' and the 'social fracture' dividing and disorienting France.

The 'crisis of confidence of citizens in their institutions', warned the Assembly's working group, stemmed from the 'absence of clarity' in the relationship between politics and money, and this 'contributes to undermine the foundations of democracy and the Republic'. In the appeal of the '103' judges to President Chirac and Prime Minister Jospin, nearly three years later, the same theme was endorsed: 'Civic morality, the essential guarantee of the democratic functioning of our society, is at risk through the proliferation of affairs.' For these 'affairs' reveal the gulf that exists between citizens and institutions (*Le Monde*, 16 July 1997).

The significance of the divide separating citizens from their 'representatives' was clearly apparent in the judgment of the criminal court of Lyon, which confirmed the conviction for corruption of a former minister in the Balladur government, Alain Carignon, also mayor of Grenoble. Corruption by business interests, according to the verdict, proceeds 'through the mad spiralling effect of money' to infect both the economic and the political world.

Yet Carignon's symbolic 'betrayal' of trust was at the heart of the matter. By 'selling part of his power to private groups' in return for financial advantages, the court declared, the mayor and former minister had committed the most serious act of corruption, which 'profoundly harms the values of the Republic' and undermines the confidence of citizens in the administration of a city and in politics itself (*Le Monde*, 18 November 1995).

The judges themselves, however, are not always consistent in their attitude towards corruption. Thus, in one recent case, the criminal chamber of the Court of Appeal (*Cour de Cassation*) was asked to judge the action of a certain chief executive, who ten years previously had provided 760,000 francs to Pierre Botton, son-in-law of the then minister of external trade, Michel Noir (also mayor of Lyon). The minister was asked to reduce the fiscal debt of the executive's company, then amounting to 15 million francs. This was quickly done. The minister, in a letter to the chief executive in September 1987, stated that he had 'personally studied' the dossier and that he intended to reduce the debt by 10 million francs because of the 'efforts made' by the company (reported by Anne Chemin, *Le Monde*, 8 February 1997).

This act of bribery was not corrupt, decided the Court of Appeal, in the form of an 'abuse of social goods'. (The 'abuse' is the 'ill faith' of a director, acting contrary to the interests of the company, so that the

director benefits personally or so that another company in which the
director has an interest benefits.) The reason for the Court's judgment was
simple: the 'commission' paid by the director to the minister was not an
'abuse' because it was not contrary to the interests of the company! This
complacent opinion was qualified, some months later, by the decision
(concerning the Carignon case) of another judge in the criminal chamber
of the Court of Appeal (reported by Maurice Peyrot, *Le Monde*,
29 October 1997). The Court in this case argued that corruption, even if
advantageous in the short term, harms the 'credit and reputation' of the
company involved.

The underlying problem, however, is that of French law. Unlike the
situation in Anglo-Saxon countries, the law prescribes a time limit for prosecutions: a ten-year period for a crime, three years for an 'offence' (*délit*)
and one year for an 'infraction' (*contravention*). 'Abuse of social goods' is an
offence and its time limit begins at the moment when the abuse has been
declared by the courts – in the above case, after Michel Noir's own appeal
against conviction had been rejected in January 1996.

The paradox is this: 'abuse of social goods' is difficult to prove (because
the company may indeed benefit from giving bribes) but it is easy to prose-
cute because of the period when the time limit begins. The offence of
'corruption', on the contrary, is in theory easy to prove (when a person
holding a position of public authority accepts or solicits certain 'advantages' in order to carry out, or not carry out, his or her functions: such
advantages include the payment of money or its equivalent); but in practice 'corruption' is difficult to prove: the time limit for prosecution starts
from the period when the offence was committed, not when it was discov-
ered (which may be years later, and therefore exempt from prosecution).
Moreover, the Court of Appeal has insisted on a 'cause–effect' link
between gift (or promise) and action (or non-action); and there must be a
prior 'pact of corruption' if the gift follows the corrupt deed. Except in the
most blatant cases, such a pact is difficult to prove.

Commenting on the earlier (Botton–Noir) affair in its editorial of
8 February 1997, *Le Monde* contrasted with striking effect the solemn
announcement by President Chirac, two weeks earlier, on the need for the
reform of justice with the judicial decision on the 'abuse of social goods',
which permitted acts of bribery as long as the enterprise benefited.
Significantly, *Le Monde* had just published (31 January 1997) the findings of
an opinion poll, which was extremely critical of the judicial system: 82 per
cent of those polled considered that justice was subject to political power;
73 per cent thought that justice was more indulgent to politicians than to
ordinary citizens; 69 per cent felt the same about high officials. These

opinions were shared almost equally among those on the Right as on the Left.

Indeed, on 22 January 1997, Chirac had rightly declared that 'the way in which justice is rendered and the way in which it is experienced by citizens lies at the heart of democracy. There can be no State of law, no Republican virtue, without good justice.' In contrast, as *Le Monde* pointed out, the Court of Appeal's decision in the Botton–Noir case – 'in effect, a kind of legalization of corrupt practices' – could only create consternation among supporters of democracy.

It is only realistic to emphasize, accordingly, the real threat of corruption in an imperfect democracy. For, despite the claims of democratic theory, the 'people' are not sovereign. First, they have only intermittent control over their elected representatives, who tend to form a distinct political class. Second, the function of the 'elect' is not so much to carry out the wishes of the electorate as to mediate the interests of society and the interests of the economy. To satisfy the former is desirable (more than desirable during elections); to satisfy the latter, essential. Such 'collusion' between political and economic elites is the normal practice of affairs.

Now, whatever its 'developmental' efficacy, corruption disturbs this precarious exchange relationship, established by democratic institutions, between wealth and power. When corruption – going beyond collusion – is 'normalized' by the political class it signifies the perversion of this relationship. As a result, citizens are either alienated from the 'system' or, what is worse, also seek to benefit, to the degree available to them, from the opportunities of corruption ('everybody does it'). When such a state of corruption is accepted as normal in society then the crucial institutional mediation between people, politicians and business – however imperfect a form of democratic practice – is destroyed.

References

Girling, J. (1997) *Corruption, Capitalism and Democracy*, London: Routledge.
Hamilton, A. (1961) *The Federalist Papers*, intro. C. Rossiter, New York: New American Library.
Kennedy, G. (ed.) (1949) *Democracy and the Gospel of Wealth*, Boston: D.C. Heath.
Mény, Y. (1992) *La corruption de la République*, Paris: Fayard.
Le Monde, various.
Projet (1992–3) no. 232, 'Attention Corruption!'
Weber, M. (1958) *The Protestant Ethic and the Spirit of Capitalism*, trans. T. Parsons, New York: Scribners.

9   Civil society

La même tornade que les évènements avaient déchainée sur la presse
secouait les milieux littéraires et artistiques. Les écrivains, en particulier, du
fait de leur vocation de connaître et d'exprimer l'homme . . . .Car, dans les
lettres, comme en tout, le talent est un titre de responsabilité.

Charles de Gaulle

The formation of 'civil society' everywhere is an integral part of the
process of modernization. It is directly related to economic growth, on the
one hand, and to the founding of pluralist politics, on the other. An influential civil society helps to counter the repressive tendencies both of
political power and of economic power. These are the 'general conditions'
of civil society – analysed in more detail below – which naturally take on
different forms, according to the specific historical, social or cultural developments in any given country. Thus in France, historically, the state has
been powerful and civil society correspondingly weak and fragmented.
Currently, however, this situation is being reversed.

'Civil society' conveys the sense of 'responsibility' of these intermediate
groups and associations – asserting autonomy from the state and the
economic system – which (ideally) transform *particular* interests, whether
environmental, feminist, generational, professional or academic, into the
general interest: namely, the voice of citizens. A mature and effective civil
society is the necessary counterpart to the imperatives of market capitalism, the imperfection of political institutions and the exigencies of the
state.

The peculiarity of civil society in France, however, is that the role of
intellectuals has traditionally been strong (from the Enlightenment to the
Existentialists), while that of other components of civil society (from environmentalists to feminists) has been weak, notably in comparison with
other European countries.

Thus, the peace movement in France, unlike the nuclear disarmers in

Britain and the militant pacifists in Germany, hardly caused a sleepless night to the Gaullist partisans of grandeur and the exalted state. Even the Socialists came round to accepting the nuclear *force de frappe*. (The peace movement in France was too long appropriated as an instrument of policy by the Communist Party: S. Hazareesingh, *Political Traditions in Modern France*, 198–201.) Environmentalists, late on the scene, were in turn 'fragilized' by personal rivalries and ideological disputes: whether to be 'pure' and stand apart from the established political scene or be 'pragmatic' by allying with sympathetic parties and thus seek to influence power.

As for the media, the circulation of serious newspapers is small (less than half that of their counterparts in Britain or in Germany) and the price is high; conversely, the 'mass media' (such as television and radio) purvey their message, as everywhere else, widely and commercially. Feminism, like the quality press, for years made little impact on established ways of thinking and behaving. (Read Simone de Beauvoir's account of the male reaction – 'violent and base' – to her pioneering study, *Le Deuxième Sexe*.) Generationally, on the other hand, changes in the family, marriage (and non-marriage), divorce rates, households (women going to work), leisure activities, 'youth culture', etc., have swept all before them.

Even trade unions, despite sporadic militancy, have traditionally been weak (at present representing only about one worker in ten) and fragmented (politically divided). Ironically, their condition is not unlike that of the Catholic Church today, once so powerful in the life of ordinary citizens and so controversial politically.

But France, too, is converging towards European norms. The influence of intellectuals, in line with 'postmodernist' theorizing (see Chapter 11, 'Culture'), is now diffuse and even dissipated. Conversely, environmentalism and feminism, strongly represented in the Jospin government, have at last come into their own.

In this chapter, I first analyse the general characteristics of civil society. Then I consider French 'specificity': the role of intellectuals during the Cold War and the Algerian crisis; the 'events' of 1968; and the mobilization of intellectuals in protest against neo-Gaullist immigration policies. Finally, I review changes in the other components of civil society: have these 'particular interests' crystallized into the 'general interest'?

Character of civil society

Civil society, as noted above, includes members of the liberal professions, civic associations, religious bodies, political parties, educational institutions (from students to teachers), the media, trade unions and, not least, non-governmental organizations. Directly corresponding to economic

development is the growth in the 'intermediate' forces of civil society –
notably in their capacity as professionals, organizers and intellectuals.

Hence the threefold, progressive character of civil society:

1   it is a product of economic development, which creates a need for
    more and more architects, economists, lawyers, accountants and, in
    turn, more and more teachers and professors to 'produce' them;
2   civil society emerges in reaction to the *existing* form of state power and
    of the economic system;
3   starting from a position of dependence on state and economy, civil
    society increasingly asserts its autonomy. Members of civil society, as
    citizens, insist on having a say in the formation of public policies,
    economic and political, which determine the way they live.

It is precisely in this intermediary role that civil society faces the state:
that is, the controllers of state power in its coercive, fiscal, legal, administrative and cultural (educational) aspects; and the way in which power is
manifested at any given time. In so far as the state has a unifying impact
(its branches are coordinated by a sense of class interest or discipline, status
or public service) it will react to the challenge of civil society with a variety
of methods, ranging from intimidation or manipulation (e.g. of the media)
to indifference or contempt (in regard to intellectuals) or even the offer of
co-operation (to professionals and organizers) in a new division of labour.

Just as the state is a mechanism for organizing individuals and groups
according to a hierarchical principle (allocating order, providing arbitration or justice, extracting and distributing wealth, ensuring social
conformity through education and propaganda), so the capitalist system of
production, distribution and exchange also structures members of society,
each day and every day, for a major part of their existence, either as
workers or managers, producers or consumers: all bringing to the market-
place the assets that they have, or do not have. Civil society is a (symbolic)
intruder into these two great organized spheres of existence.

Hence the contradictory nature of civil society. Professionals, organizers
and intellectuals were brought into being to serve the direct or indirect
needs of an expanding and ever more complex economy and polity. But
the changed society brought about by their entry becomes all the more
different – and distant – from the old patterns of power and wealth, which
persist, uneasily or contradictorily, with the new.

In addition, the more successful the professionals, organizers and intellectuals are in 'modernizing' society, polity and economy, the more the
different components of civil society themselves tend to diverge. So long as
'citizens' had a common interest in struggling against the old order the

solidarity of civil society was assured: for it was inspired by a vision of a society that was not dominated by the traditional elite and was not exploited by capitalists at the 'primitive' stage of accumulation.

But with the effective assertion of autonomy – the recognition of a role for civil society by the more 'liberal' state and the more 'mature' economy – new material interests in civil society come to the fore. The more conservative professionals and organizers increasingly identify themselves with the economic and political structures that sustain them; the more progressive professionals and intellectuals increasingly identify themselves with the struggle of the poor and the powerless – either for a better stake in society (reformers) or for a total change of society (revolutionaries).

Nevertheless, despite the centrifugal forces of Left and Right a substantial intermediate group remains. New activities in civil society led by this group (or the reformers) may be non-political in objective (such as protection of the environment or women's rights) but require political action or influence to be effective. Indeed, such activities bring in the participatory element of democracy in a far more direct way than is possible in the representative style of democracy, with its docile or intermittent participation of citizens (i.e. during elections). Here the impetus of reform renews the inspiration of civil society (John Girling, section on civil society in *Corruption, Capitalism and Democracy*, 164–6).

Role of intellectuals: revolution or reform

Socialism and the Soviet Union

Jean-Paul Sartre and Simone de Beauvoir were the most widely admired intellectuals of their time: in her memoirs, *La Force des choses*, Simone de Beauvoir gives an extraordinary picture of the intense, frenzied, confused, exciting, creative and combative struggle by themselves and other intellectuals, confronted with the Cold War, to 'engage' with one side or the other.

Sartre, Beauvoir, Maurice Merleau-Ponty (their 'phenomenalist' ally), for a time 'objective' supporters of the Soviet Union, were derided by the French Communist Party under its Stalinist leaders, distrusted by Camus, their former close companion, and criticized by Raymond Aron, prewar friend and postwar intellectual spokesman for the Right. (See Aron, *Marxism and the Existentialists*: Sartre, he writes, is more moralist than sociologist, seeking to reconcile the philosophy of personal destiny with the Marxist philosophy of collective salvation by history.) Merleau-Ponty, in the early years of the Cold War, published *Le Yogi et le Prolétaire* against Arthur Koestler's anti-Stalinist *The Yogi and the Commissar*.

According to Merleau-Ponty, the objective reality of our acts escapes us, but it is on these acts that we will be judged, not on our intentions. Thus, when the Soviet Union in 1936 (the year of the show trial of the former Bolshevik leader, Bukharin) was isolated and threatened it could only save the revolution at the cost of 'monolithic rigour'. Then the objective face of opposition (as with Bukharin) amounted to treason. Merleau-Ponty subordinated morality to history (objective reality). 'We jumped ahead with him,' writes Simone de Beauvoir, 'conscious, without yet being detached from it, that moralism was the last citadel of bourgeois idealism' (*La Force des choses*, 121).

This stance displeased Camus. He was at the time far from being a Gaullist, but he was still further from the Communist Party. Having just returned from the United States, though with less sympathy for America than Sartre showed on his visit, Camus remained hostile to the Soviet Union. One day Sartre reproached Camus for 'too much morality, not enough politics' in his editorials for the progressive newspaper *Combat*, which drew protests from Camus. Sartre's existentialist profundity in any case irritated Camus: he preferred 'French clarity' instead. As Beauvoir observed: 'Our relations remained very cordial, but from far away a shadow obscured them: this was due much more to Camus than to Sartre or me.'

A newcomer, with 'tumultuous personality', then erupted on the scene: Koestler himself. At once he told Sartre: 'You are a better novelist than I am, but less good as a philosopher.' Explaining his theory of physiological materialism, Koestler embarrassed his hosts by his 'heavily autodidactic manner', his doctrinaire assurance and his 'scientism derived from a mediocre Marxist formation'. When they were with Camus no one spoke of their books, but Koestler was always demanding, 'Read what I have written about it.' Success had gone to his head (Beauvoir, 122–3).

One day Koestler invited Sartre, Beauvoir and Camus (with whom he was closely linked) to a night club, the day before Sartre was due to give a lecture at the Sorbonne, sponsored by UNESCO, on 'the responsibility of the writer'! Koestler ordered zakuski, vodka and champagne. Although Sartre had not prepared his lecture, and counted on going home early to do so, 'alcohol, gipsy music and the ardour of our conversation soon made us lose all control of time'. Camus repeated a theme dear to him: 'If one could only write the truth!' At the same time Koestler insisted that it was impossible to be friends if one did not agree politically. He reproached Sartre and even Camus for allying with Stalin. Camus retorted to Beauvoir: 'What we have in common is that individuals come first; we prefer the concrete to the abstract, people to doctrines, and friendship to politics.' All, apart from Koestler, agreed 'with an emotion heightened by alcohol and the late hour'. Sartre slept two or three hours, and then stuffed himself with a stimulant to prepare his lecture.

Such was the atmosphere of intellectual life. The political content was more controversial. Sartre's 'commitment' to the Soviet Union at the height of the Cold War derived from what he saw as the logic of Socialism. Taken as a whole, the Socialist movement, he later wrote, 'is the absolute judge of all others, because the exploited confront exploitation and the class struggle as their reality, exposing the truth of bourgeois societies'. Moreover, Socialism is 'the movement of man in the course of making himself, while other political parties believe that man is already made. To understand a political enterprise, socialism is the absolute reference.'

Despite everything, Simone de Beauvoir insisted in the early years of the Cold War, the USSR is and remains the country of Socialism: the revolutionary seizure of power has been achieved.

> Even if the bureaucracy is stratified, if the police have accumulated enormous power, if crimes have been committed, the USSR has never called into question the appropriation of the means of production; its regime differs radically from those aiming to establish or maintain class domination.
>
> (p. 218)

Yet the Revolution has been betrayed, disfigured, so people say. 'No', Sartre replied. 'The Revolution is incarnate, that is to say, the universal has entered into the particular.' Once achieved, it soon fell into the contradictions which separated it from its conceptual purity; 'but Russian socialism had in regard to the dream of a stainless socialism the immense advantage of already existing' (p. 219) – the 'already existing' Socialism that was later to be the subject of well-founded critiques.

What are we to make of this obstinate attachment to the Soviet Union? Unlike Camus, for Sartre the 'abstract' has overridden the 'concrete'. Sartre was carried away by the Hegelian notion of the 'universal' as the ultimate Reality, while the empirical world (of power and repression) is mere appearance and particularity. For Sartre, Socialism – the world of the future – was 'incarnated' in the Soviet Union: it cannot be repudiated, for it is 'immanent', in the very process of fulfilment.

As for Beauvoir, collective appropriation of production existed in the Soviet Union: a fundamental achievement that overrides 'secondary' concerns. This was an illusion. As was evident at the time, the state had appropriated the economy, and the *nomenklatura* (the Soviet elite) appropriated the state. Any misgivings that Sartre and Beauvoir might have had were simply suppressed for the sake of a higher reality – in other words, faith. A lively discussion of the intellectual world – with profiles of Sartre, Beauvoir, Camus, Aron, Mauriac, Malraux and others in 'The Age of Sartre' – is given by Michel Winock in *Le Siècle des intellectuels*. As he notes, it was not until the Soviet suppression of the Hungarian revolution in 1956 that Sartre broke with his Soviet friends and with the French Communist Party.

Algeria

In contrast to the doctrinaire and flawed opinions of Sartre and Beauvoir with regard to the Soviet Union, their stance over Algeria was principled, consistent, far-sighted and courageous. From the beginning of the Algerian struggle for independence, Beauvoir noted that Mendès France had sent reinforcements, his successor Edgar Faure refused to negotiate, the police in Algeria imprisoned and tortured, and the army swore never to abandon Algeria.

The humiliating capitulation of Guy Mollet, the Socialist prime minister, to the army and French colonists left Sartre and Beauvoir stupefied. Mollet had been elected to put an end to the 'cruel and stupid' war; instead he intensified it. He attempted to justify his reversal of policy by all-out propaganda, claiming that the Algerian people loved France, and that the revolt was the product of an 'Islamic conspiracy' headed by Nasser.

The press in turn concealed the reality of repression in Algeria by lies and silences. Critics were treated as 'traitors' stabbing the mother-country in the back. Sartre even urged the pro-Communist 'Peace Movement' to condemn the Algerian war; but a Soviet delegate declared this would be 'inopportune'. The Peace Movement only opposed wars of aggression; and France was not an aggressor. As for the French Communist Party, it feared to cut itself off from the masses if it appeared less nationalistic than the other parties; it made no effort to combat the racism of French workers (*La Force des choses*, 360–2).

The whole country was foundering in chauvinism and racism. Sartre and Beauvoir were accused of demoralizing the nation. Why should this be so, she asked? 'Childhood, youth, language, culture, interests, all attached us to France.' Their 'powerless and saddening isolation' over Algeria was not at all to be envied. 'And yet it was imposed on us because we were aware of the evidence.' For the war was condemning hundreds and thousands of Algerians to suffering and death, while in France 'it demanded a systematic mystification of opinion, the suffocation of liberty, perversion of ideologies, the corruption of a country stuffed with lies to the point of losing all sense of truth' (p. 363).

By 1957, three years after the outbreak of the war, the evidence of murder and torture could no longer be concealed: 'bones broken, faces and genitals burnt, nails pulled off, bodies impaled . . . entire battalions pillaged, burned, violated, massacred. Torture was employed as a normal and essential way of getting information; it was not a matter of accidents, or excesses, but a system.' The campaign led by the Left against torture could not be ignored by French opinion, which embarrassed the government. Even the Church could no longer avoid the issue; but none of the bishops was prepared to condemn it (pp. 389–90, 402, 405–6).

De Gaulle, in power, spoke for the first time of 'self-determination' for Algeria. And yet, even during the course of negotiations, Michelet, the minister of justice, admitted to Simone de Beauvoir:

'It is terrible, this gangrene [torture] which the Nazis introduced. It invades everything, it corrupts everything, it cannot be eliminated. Beating-up, that's normal: no police without beating-up [*passage à tabac*]; but torture! I try to get them to understand that there is a line that must not be crossed.' He raised his shoulders to indicate his helplessness. 'It is a gangrene,' he repeated. 'Fortunately, it is all going to end.'

(p. 527)

It was not quite the end. After the 1962 agreement on independence for Algeria, those who condemned it (the OAS, the secret army organization) launched a campaign of terror against de Gaulle and those, like Sartre and Beauvoir, who had consistently supported independence. 'Most journalists, politicians, writers and academics on the Left were victims of attacks.' The OAS even exploded a bomb in Sartre's apartment: he could never return (Beauvoir, 639, 641. And see Winock on the intellectuals and Algeria, 512–45).

1968

Unlike the protracted struggle over Algeria, the 'events' of May 1968 were perhaps the single most dramatic incident of the century in France. For a few delirious, exhilarating weeks students and workers 'detonated' the outdated traditions, the hierarchical authority, the rigid controls, the stifling attitudes of the 'old order' and in a spontaneous liberating movement voiced the generous (if confused) aspirations of the people to create their own free associations for a new, generous and humane society. It could not last. In an equally extraordinary and just as rapid reversal of fortunes, the old order reasserted its 'constitutional' hegemony. Yet the memory of those days of boundless freedom and almost unbelievable achievements retains its hold even today.

The 'events' of May exemplified to an uncanny degree the thesis of a brilliant revolutionary theorist, companion-in-arms of Che Guevara, Régis Debray. Analysing the success of the Cuban revolution, Debray argued (*Revolution in the Revolution?*) that the 'insurrectionary centre' (the *foco*), organized by professional revolutionaries, acts as a 'detonator' precisely at the point where the regime is at its weakest; it is designed to explode at the most favourable moment. The myth of the *foco* electrifies the masses: it emits shock waves of energy and enlightenment, which galvanize the people into awareness and action.

What was exceptional for Latin America – the detonating achievement in Cuba of a tiny minority of determined revolutionaries – Debray made into a rule (with fatal results: Guevara himself was killed in 1967 trying to establish a *foco* in Bolivia). Conversely, the student revolution that was common to most industrialized countries in 1968 – in Germany, the United States and Japan, for example – in France was exceptional in its scope: the movement of workers and students developed in an unprecedented way. For Sartre, the students extended the field of possibilities: they 'put imagination in power'. For Aron, on the contrary, it was a 'psychodrama' (Winock, 565, 567, and see Aron, *Le spectateur engagé*, 255–71; on Sartre and the Left, 'The opium of the intellectuals', 174–91).

The 1968 events, as Serge Berstein reports, expressed the 'moral and social crisis' of France: the inadequacy of traditional values and behaviour in face of the new realities brought about by economic and social change. Students refused to accept the alienation of people resulting from the unremitting emphasis on 'productivist ideology': that is, financial profitability at all costs and consumerism to the utmost.

Student activists rejected all forms of authority, whether of the state, economic enterprises, family, religion, or traditional morality. They demanded the right to happiness as the fundamental virtue crowning freedom. But to achieve the revolution of personality (personal fulfilment) as well as that of society (meeting social demands through collective decisions) necessitated a 'permanent contestation' of the bourgeoisie (Berstein, *La France de l'expansion*, 301–3).

The immediate conditions of the student revolt were the massive increase in student numbers (from 200,000 to half a million from 1960 to 1968) and the inadequate facilities in buildings, staff and degree courses. University lecture theatres, where there was no room to sit and where students sometimes had to take notes in the corridors, became the rule. Meanwhile, the newly hired junior staff, known as *maîtres-assistants*, disliked their subordinate status and felt their jobs were precarious. As for the students, under the open-admissions system between one-third and half failed to get degrees. Finally, the issue of unemployment loomed all the more seriously for those who graduated.

The extreme-Left activists – a heady mixture of Trotskyites, Maoists, 'spontaneists', anarchists and 'Sorbonne Marxists' – argued that the university, under such conditions, was merely a cog-wheel in the techno-cratic state, whose function was to train people to serve the capitalist system. The students, they insisted, should not seek to be integrated into this corrupt society, but they should contest it – by direct action. In this way, student provocations would force the authorities to reveal their 'true' repressive character, which in turn would alienate the mass of the people, transforming them into revolutionaries (Berstein, 305–8; Patrick Seale and Maureen McConville, *French Revolution 1968*, 21–3, 31–2, 35; Antoine Prost, *Education, société et politiques*, 134–47).

These tactics succeeded to perfection. Student occupation of universi-ties in Paris provoked the authorities to send in the police, who behaved with great brutality. (See the horrifying eye-witness reports cited by the student union, UNEF, and university teachers' union, SNESup: SNESup, *Le Livre noir des journées de mai*.) Police brutality generated an enormous movement of solidarity for the embattled students – a movement which spread throughout the provinces and, in turn, ignited rebellion among the workers, equally dissatisfied with the customary authoritarianism of factory bosses and their own, deteriorating, economic conditions.

Without a national word of command, strikes spread across the country, spontaneously, like a contagion. By the end of May, ten million workers were on strike, equally in the private sector as the public, among junior and mid-level executives as among the mass of workers. The unions were caught by surprise: the pro-Communist CGT, fearful of Leftist 'adven-turism', vainly tried to channel a movement escaping their control; only the Catholic-oriented CFTD sympathized with the social as well as economic demands of the strikers. Workers sought a change in personal relations, contesting hierarchical authority, and insisted on free expression of views and collective decisions – thus identifying themselves with the libertarian and social appeal of the students (Berstein, 310–11; Seale and McConville, 145–56).

Equally caught by surprise, the government was slow to react. Only towards the end of the month, after Prime Minister Pompidou had granted major concessions to the workers, did President de Gaulle, in a televised speech to the nation, reverse the course of events. This was the decisive moment. The 'silent majority' was by now fearful that events were out of control, they were tired of the continuing disturbances, of the incessant speeches, and they were beginning to suffer materially from the strikes. To them, de Gaulle reaffirmed the authority of the state; he played on their fears of a 'Communist plot' and promised a return to normality. In the general elections held at the end of June 1968, the Right had a landslide victory; the Left, confused and uncertain, suffered a historic loss (Berstein, 313–23).

Civil disobedience 1997

Another spontaneous movement, inspired by civic consciousness, had a happier outcome: but this was in protest over a single issue and did not seek to repudiate the entire system of authority, as in 1968. The issue was the reinforcement by the Juppé government in February 1997 of already very strict immigration controls (the Pasqua laws of 1993). Under pressure from Right-wing deputies and in a transparent attempt to steal the thunder from Le Pen's National Front, the minister of the interior, Jean-Louis Debré, demanded that citizens should inform the authorities of any breach in the laws by immigrants.

Two film-makers first went public with their refusal to 'inform' on people subject to 'unjust' laws, and they were soon joined by others in the 'Appeal of the 121' (a symbolic number: the same as for the protest against the Algerian war). According to the Appeal, the National Assembly had voted a law which would 'suppress the essential rights of the men and women of this country'. The signatories declared that they were 'guilty of having recently sheltered foreigners in an irregular situation . . . . and we shall continue to shelter them – and not denounce them – to sympathize and work with our colleagues and friends without verifying their papers.'

The number of signatories increased rapidly: along with film-makers there were writers, theatre directors, artists, doctors, architects, social workers, psychologists, musicians, journalists, lawyers and academics – a veritable inventory of civil society! But neither the Socialist leader, Lionel Jospin, nor the Communist chief, Robert Hue, were to be found among their numbers (*Le Monde*, 16–17 February 1997).

Three-quarters of those supporting the Appeal, according to an opinion poll, considered that the Socialist Party was not sufficiently committed to opposing the immigration laws, and more than half felt the same about the Communist Party (*Le Monde*, 25 February 1997). As on previous occasions, leaders of the Left were reluctant to give a lead, even on such issues of principle, for fear of alienating their traditional supporters. Indeed, a poll published by *Libération* on 20 February indicated that 59 per cent of those interviewed favoured the government's immigration controls. Thus, it was left to members of civil society, and not the 'responsible' politicians, to give a lead.

Inevitably, the Appeal to disobedience aroused controversy, especially on the Right. A sceptical intellectual, Emmanuel Todd, although disapproving of the Debré law, complained that there was 'something perverse' about a movement of 'cultural elites' which concentrated on immigration and not on matters that really affected 'popular circles', such as high unemployment and exclusion (interview, *Le Monde*, 16–17 February 1997). Todd, like those on the Right who argued in the same vein, missed the point. The Appeal was against an 'unjust' law; the signatories were trying to mobilize opinion so as to have it changed. They may well be opposed to high unemployment *as well*; but they were concerned with a different, and far from trivial, issue.

The theme of a higher morality in contradiction with 'positive' law was invoked by the philosopher Etienne Balibar ('Democratic state of emergency', *Le Monde*, 19 February 1997). Such, he wrote, are the values – hospitality, the truth, inviolability of human beings – that enable a political community to speak of justice and rights, which a government or state must safeguard at all costs. When there is a contradiction between these values and particular laws it is the duty of citizens to express themselves publicly, by proclaiming their obedience to such higher 'unwritten' laws, even to the detriment of actual legislation.

Disobedience, however, must be subject to certain conditions, Balibar argued. There must be a 'situation of emergency', when a threshold has been crossed in the degradation of the state; when civil disobedience, always resting upon individual initiatives, offers the possibility of collective action to change the law in question; and when those disobeying accept the consequences of their action. When such conditions are met they create the necessary counterpart to the arbitrariness of power – the democratic equivalent of the state of emergency.

The offending clause in the immigration legislation was later removed. But the Jospin government's 'balanced' review of the immigration and nationality acts (and its decision not to abrogate the original Pasqua laws) met with disapproval by the petitioners.

Strengths and weaknesses of civil society

The media

Newspaper readership is relatively small in France: 182 readers of the daily press per thousand population, compared with 582 in Japan, 330 in Britain, 318 in Germany and 297 in the United States (*World Press Trends*,

June 1997). Among the quality newspapers, *Le Monde* is unsurpassed: it is also most read by businesspeople. Three-quarters of a million owners and executives read *Le Monde* regularly, ahead of the economic daily *Les Echos*, the sporting *L'Equipe*, *Le Figaro* (equivalent of the *Daily Telegraph*) and the Left-leaning *Libération* (Ipsos survey, June 1997).

Its business readership does not preserve *Le Monde* from economic pressures. '*Le Monde* is formed in an incessant battle against two adversaries', declared its editor, Jean-Marie Colombani, on its fiftieth anniversary (September 1994). These are: 'money, in its claim to be the sole judge of human success'; therefore the paper has to struggle for its independence. The other enemy is time, that is immediacy, when the paper must struggle to distance itself from events. 'Virtue, rigour, liberty and responsibility' are required in this task – as also in confrontation with yet another adversary: the aim by the system of power to impose its own controlled information. (Nevertheless, a recent opinion poll, reported by Anne Chemin in *Le Monde*, 7 October 1997, showed considerable scepticism by most French people as to the reliability of information in the press and, in particular, their hostility to investigative journalism.)

Yet for a quality journal, economic power poses the greatest danger to freedom, reiterated Colombani (interview, *Marianne*, 28 April–4 May 1997). While it is considered legitimate for the media to criticize politics, this does not extend to economics, especially the power of large groups, which have emerged after restructuring in the last fifteen years. These bosses do not accept criticism. (The then chief of Alcatel, one of the largest French firms, simply removed its publicity budget from *Le Monde*. It was the largest contributor: four million francs a year.) But industrial groups taking over newspapers are still more dangerous: 'At any given time, these newspapers are seen to be instruments of influence or as an element in a communications strategy.'

As for French television, commercialization long ran second to the 'influence of power' as the major threat to freedom of expression. Only in 1982, with the advent of a Socialist government, was the state monopoly of television ended. For nearly forty years before this, opposition leaders got little or no television coverage, while the news was regularly vetted by government ministers. 'Censorship was direct: each morning there was a meeting with the minister to draw up the news agenda'! During the 1968 events, for example, television coverage, unlike that of the other media, initially supported the government and failed to report the extent of the revolt (Sheila Perry, 'Television', *Aspects of Contemporary France*, 116–17).

It was under Mitterrand, however, that commercialization took over. Commentators generally agree, Perry notes, that the competition for advertising revenues leads to uniform programmes. The aim of a company run on commercial lines is to make a profit which, if not precluding quality, aims to satisfy the greatest number, rather than minority groups; it thus runs counter to the ethos of public service broadcasting. (See also my Chapter 11 on commercialized culture.)

'Ours is a commercial channel', confirmed Francis Bouygues, the new owner of the privatized first channel (TF1). 'There are things we do not wish to do, such as broadcast cultural, political or educational programmes.' The second and third channels are still publicly owned, but both compete for ratings with the commercial channels. As Perry puts it (p. 124), economic pressures mean that cultural and other minority programmes are relegated to less popular viewing times, since channels cannot afford to devote prime time, when the audience is largest, to minority groups.

Yet another consequence of competing for a mass audience, wrote two journalists with France 2 (*Le Monde*, 5 July 1997), is the failure of public television adequately to inform. 'One shows everything, one agitates, one explains very little.' Describing the world as if it were a cartoon story, addressed to spectators rather than to citizens, is to produce a caricature of events. How is it possible to resist such harmful trends, they ask, when the state-shareholder of France 2 reduces its budget and obliges it to appeal to advertising interests for 50 per cent of its funding?

Feminism

A very different problem is brought out by Simone de Beauvoir's pioneering work, *Le Deuxième Sexe*, which was first published in 1949. Wishing to write about herself, she found she had to write about the female condition. She discussed the myths that men had created through cosmologies, religions, superstitions, ideologies and literatures. In all cases, man presented himself as the Subject and considered woman as an Object, as the Other. So far from removing all distinctions between men and women, she showed that such differences were cultural and not natural.

The first volume (history, myths, formation) was well received. The second (the situation of women, justifications and 'towards liberation') created a scandal. She was stupefied by the reaction. Apart from her immediate circle of friends, Sartre, Merleau-Ponty, Leiris, the sculptor Giacometti and others, men reproached her for 'obscenity' (one would believe that Freud and psycho-analysis had never existed). She received, signed or anonymous, satirical epistles, exhortations and warnings. She was treated as 'unsatisfied, cold, priapic, nymphomaniac, lesbian . . . .The violence of these reactions and their lowness' left her perplexed. Catholicism, it is true, among latin peoples encouraged masculine tyranny and even inclined it towards sadism. But even among friends, a progressive academic refused to read any further, while Camus accused her of making the French male ridiculous! Those on the Right could only detest her book. Rome put it on the forbidden list. Marxists were hardly more helpful: once the Revolution had taken place, they said, the 'woman problem' would no longer exist (*La Force des choses*, 203–11).

Beauvoir's courageous work in time has had an effect. With the rise of feminism after 1968, the women's liberation movement (MLF) was created two years later. *Choisir*, founded by Beauvoir and the lawyer Gisèle Halimi in 1972, successfully campaigned for the availability of contraception in 1974 and the legalization of abortion (Simone Veil's bill) in 1975; and generally in defence of the legal rights of women. Yet, as Charlot points out, feminist movements, like others in civil society, do not meet the impartial arbitration of the state, but rather one that is implicated in the play of interests: the political power of the moment often favours the groups aligned with it at the expense of groups considered hostile to its ideas and policies (*La politique en France*, 242).

Moreover, despite the principle of equality between men and women, the latter are in practice still disadvantaged, especially at work. Women make up 44 per cent of the work force (indeed, 77 per cent of those aged between 25 and 49 work outside the household). They do so because an extra salary is important and because it affords women real autonomy and fulfilment. Yet women are mainly concentrated in the service sector, in low-status, low-paid, less secure jobs. There is also a growing gap between (middle-class) women with qualifications, whose conditions of work are similar to men's, and women without qualifications (working-class) whose lives are characterized by insecurity and unemployment. Further, 25 per cent of women are on part-time work, compared with only 4 per cent of men (Alison Holland, 'Women' in Perry, ed., *Aspects of Contemporary France*, 139–40).

On average, women earn considerably less than men: 24 per cent less in 1994. In 1985, only half of all women graduates obtained managerial posts, compared with three-quarters of men. Currently, about 30 per cent of top jobs are held by women. Yet there is not a single woman at the head of one of the 200 biggest companies in France. Even in the civil service, less than 6 per cent of the most senior administrative posts are held by women, under 3 per cent of prefects and less than 4 per cent of ambassadors (Holland, 140–1). Moreover, if two junior or mid-level executives out of five are women, according to Michèle Aulagnon (*Le Monde*, 5 November 1997), only one in twenty directors of firms are women. (See also Rachel Silvera on inequality of salaries, and Christine Fournier on women with degrees, *L'Etat de la France*, 91–5, 96–8.)

As for women in politics, this is 'masculine territory par excellence', writes Elisabeth Guigou, minister of justice in the Jospin government, for the entry of women is seen as a transgression of the rules. Soberly, with a mixture of rage and humiliation, Guigou traces the struggle of women like herself to end the 'lamentable French exception' which largely excludes women from politics: only one in twenty deputies were women in the National Assembly elected in 1993; and only one woman for twenty men were mayors (Gérard Courtois, review of Elisabeth Guigou, *Etre Femme en politique: Le Monde*, 25 February 1997). It is all the more to the credit of Lionel Jospin that he insisted on a quota for women candidates in the 1997 elections, against the 'conventional wisdom'; and that he gave important government appointments to Martine Aubry (employment and solidarity), Guigou (justice), and Dominique Voynet (environment).

Environment

The perverse effects of progress are revealed both in the infrastructural environment in which we work and live, and ecologically: the deadly impact of pollution. Many European cities, as Bernadette Galloux-Fournier points out, produce real ghettos for the marginalized and the excluded. The ensuing frustrations rapidly degrade the social climate and create, especially among the youth, veritable disasters. In reaction, some rehabilitation of the urban environment has occurred, and local sporting and cultural associations are encouraged, but both the sense of awareness and the means to solve social hardships are limited, even derisory, in face of the huge scale of the problem (Galloux-Fournier, *L'Histoire de l'Europe au XXe. Siècle*, 326–7).

As for the menace of pollution it is especially linked with industrialization, on the one hand, and the massive increase in use of cars, on the other. The Earth Summit at Rio in 1992 accordingly recommended urgent measures to stop the degradation of the planet, in particular the greenhouse effect of global warming due to excessive energy consumption. But countries vary greatly in the effectiveness of their policies to counter industrial and automobile pollution. While the British complained of European regulations stifling industrial growth, the Germans took systematic action to protect the environment, and the French were in between: the ecological movement was fragmented and for a time the large extent of unscathed countryside in France disarmed any sense of danger (Galloux-Fournier, 330–3).

The situation in the cities, however, is more acute: the alarming 'peaks' of air pollution in Paris in the summer of 1997 put pressure on Dominique Voynet, the militant environment minister in the Jospin government, to take effective action. Stung by the criticism of rival ecologists, she announced an important long-term programme to penalize polluting vehicles (which already benefit from large tax deductions in the case of diesel) and to favour less-polluting cars. At once the powerful road transport lobby threatened industrial action if the price of diesel was increased. It is no wonder, as *Le Monde* editorialized (24–25 August 1997), that the curve of pollution reveals the 'civic index' of a country!

Trade unions

The largest union organization, the Confédération générale du travail (CGT), was founded on the Marxist assumption of a fundamental antagonism between capitalist exploiters and the exploited proletariat, the bearer of salvation for humanity. Thus, there could be no question of class collaboration, of negotiation or permanent bargaining, representation or co-management. Instead, protest and class struggle are crucial in the movement to overthrow the capitalist system, which is doomed to destruction. Hence the condition of mutual exclusion: the CGT refuses to participate with the state in order to preserve its revolutionary purity; the state is reinforced in its authoritarian attitude towards the unions. The problem, however, is that the CGT's divisive ideology is less and less perceived as legitimate, especially since the overall discrediting of Marxism (Charlot, 233).

The reformist, originally Catholic, Confédération française démocratique du travail (CFDT), on the other hand, considers itself the bearer of a 'social project', and actively campaigned during the 1970s for the Socialist presidential candidate Mitterrand. In effect, the CFDT seeks to channel the new aspirations of workers into serving the modernization of the union movement, without abandoning social transformation. After 're-centring' in 1978, the CFDT supports dialogue rather than systematic confrontation with the existing power, whether Right or Left, so as to achieve realistic demands in a contractual fashion.

Force ouvrière (FO), the third major organization, started as a breakaway movement from the CGT, and has developed, like the CFDT, an apolitical, if not opportunist, stance.

Partly as a result of the divisions in the union movement, the proportion of union membership in the working population, always small, has slumped alarmingly: from more than 17 per cent in 1978 to less than 10 per cent in 1988; the number of declared members of the CGT has fallen from more than two million to less than one million; of the CFDT from 806,000 to 447,000; FO, on the other hand, apparently rose from 680,000 to one million (Charlot, 236–7). An assessment a year later, however, indicates 600,000 for the CGT, 470,000 for the CFDT and 500,000 for FO, which seems more realistic (Anne Stevens, *The Government and Politics of France*, 284).

The five-yearly elections for councillors of the industrial tribunals (*conseillers prud'homaux*), the only real test of strength in the private sector, showed the CGT leading in 1997 with just over one-third of votes, followed by the CFDT with one-quarter and FO with slightly more than one-fifth. Yet unions in the private sector are even more marginal than in the public sector: only about 5 per cent of the work force (Alain Beuve-Méry, *Le Monde*, 8 August 1997). On a European comparison, the unionized proportion of the work force in 1988 was estimated at 40 per cent for Italy, 34 per cent for Germany and 12 per cent (actually 9 per cent in 1990) for France (Galloux-Fournier, 112). In Britain, union membership fell catastrophically from fifteen million in 1980 to barely seven million in 1995 (*Le Monde*, 19 March 1997) – but it is still far greater than the two million union members in France. Vincent Wright aptly comments (*The Government and Politics of France*, 274): 'All the major economic and social interests of France are characterized by extreme fragmentation' – and the unions are no exception.

Universal mission

But let the intellectuals have the last word. Lecturing in Japan in 1966, Sartre produced his 'Defence of Intellectuals' (later published as *Plaidoyer pour les intellectuels*, 1968). As Michel Contat explains (*Le Monde des livres*, 1 August 1997) Sartre developed the idea that 'technicians of practical knowledge', such as doctors, engineers, lawyers and social scientists – in this chapter considered as members of civil society – do not become 'intellectuals' until they are aware of the contradiction existing within themselves between the particularity of their practice and the vocation for universality of their knowledge.

Similarly, civil society either exists because of its universal vocation – democratic citizenship – or it does not exist.

References

Aron, R. (1969) *Marxism and the Existentialists*, New York: Harper & Row.
——(1981) *Le spectateur engagé*, Paris: Juilliard.
Beauvoir, S. de (1949) *Le Deuxième Sexe*, Paris: Gallimard.
——(1963) *La Force des choses*, Paris: Gallimard.
Berstein, S. (1989) *La France de l'expansion*, vol. 1, Paris: Seuil.
Charlot, J. (1994) *La politique en France*, Paris: Fallois.

Debray, R. (1968) *Revolution in the Revolution?*, Harmondsworth: Penguin.

L'Etat de la France (1997) Paris: La Découverte.

Galloux-Fournier, B. (1995) *L'Histoire de l'Europe au XXe. siècle*, vol. 5, Paris: Complexe.

Girling, J. (1997) *Corruption, Capitalism and Democracy*, London: Routledge.

Guigou, E. (1997) *Etre femme en politique*, Paris: Plon.

Hazareesingh, S. (1994) *Political Traditions in Modern France*, Oxford: Oxford University Press.

Holland, A. (1997) 'Women' in S. Perry (ed.) *Aspects of Contemporary France*, London: Routledge.

Libération, 20 February 1997.

Marianne, 28 April–4 May 1997.

Le Monde, various.

Le Monde des livres.

Perry, S. (1997) 'Television' in S. Perry (ed.) *Aspects of Contemporary France*, London: Routledge.

Prost, A. (1997) *Education, société et politiques*, Paris: Seuil.

Sartre, J.-P. (1968) *Plaidoyer pour les intellectuels*, Paris: Gallimard.

Seale, P. and McConville, M. (1968) *French Revolution 1968*, Harmondsworth: Penguin.

SNESup (1968) *Le Livre noir des journées de mai*, Paris: Seuil.

Stevens, A. (1996) *The Government and Politics of France*, London: Macmillan.

Winock, M. (1997) *Le Siècle des intellectuels*, Paris: Seuil.

World Press Trends, June 1997.

Wright, V. (1989) *The Government and Politics of France*, London: Routledge.

Part III

Society

The 'universal' economic-political alternatives to capitalism – revolutionary Marxism and even reformist Socialism – have lost their meaning, as have conventional religious beliefs, leaving for many French people an absence of identity, a void.

French 'specificity' – that is, a distinctive way of thinking and behaving – in turn no longer provides a form of reassurance, as it did in the past, in a European and world context of rapid and often bewildering change.

Individualism, as self-reliance, persists; but it is pervaded also by the 'morose' individualism of isolated atoms, helpless in a society that is beyond their reach: the 'excluded' poor, and those who are workless and often homeless.

There is need for a new solidarity: of welfare, local initiatives, voluntary associations and the force of single issues, such as the rights of women, protection of the environment, and 'inclusion' of minorities. These issues need not be seen – as they are in the uniform, centralized, elitist French tradition – as introducing divisive, and even subversive, forms of 'sectarianism' and 'corporatism', undermining the general will; but rather as new ways to give ordinary people a stake in society.

For all the dictates of 'logic' (as in economic and political decisions: Parts I and II of this study), it is society where 'meaning' is central, with an emotionally charged content: codified as Logic and latinity in Chapter 10, Culture (high and popular) in Chapter 11, and Identity in Chapter 12: namely, the historical, social and affective factors that create France's identity and its way(s) of life.

10 Logic and latinity

La paix que nous, Français, voulions aider à bâtir d'après ce qui nous semblait être la logique et la justice, les Anglais, eux, jugeaient expédient de la traiter suivant les recettes de l'empirisme et du compromis.
Ce chef [de Gaulle] ... serait-il longtemps suivi par le peuple le plus mobile et indocile de la terre?

Charles de Gaulle

De Gaulle's 'a certain idea of France' perfectly expresses these polarities, which are complementary as well as contradictory: 'logic' or reason and 'latinity' or 'mobile' emotion:

All my life I have had a certain idea of France. This is inspired by sentiment as well as reason. Emotionally, I imagine France, naturally ... as if vowed to an eminent and exceptional destiny. Instinctively, I have the impression that Providence has created it for assured success or exemplary misfortune . . . .Yet the positive side of my mind convinces me that France is not really itself except when it is in the front rank . . . .Briefly, in my view, France cannot be France without greatness.
(Charles de Gaulle, *Mémoires de guerre – L'Appel 1940–1942*, p. 1)

'Grandeur', for de Gaulle, is indispensable to France's 'identity'. But this is questionable at the present time, when the logic of economic (and political) constraints reflects the prior needs of the global economy and the European Union. It is doubtful, too, that de Gaulle has logically distinguished between sentiment and reason. For he claims that the 'positive side' of his mind, meaning rationality, convinces him that France is 'really itself' only when it is in the front rank. A more reasonable interpretation would be that 'sentiment' (or history, or 'destiny') had so convinced him.
Rationality (cognition) – disciplined by logic (rules for valid inferences) –

provides an explanation of ourselves, society and the world. Sentiment (emotion, 'latinity') gives meaning to that existence. Is there, for example, an affective, inclusive 'society' or is there no such thing, as Thatcher claims, according to free-market logic? Such an attitude would preclude the meaningful relationship of any intermediate body between the family (considered the bedrock of traditional virtues) and the nation-state. A society-less nation is one form of identification; but, emotionally, it is more likely to inspire racism or chauvinism than the more generous form of patriotism.

It is rational to try to understand the forces at work, the 'structural' conditions, that shape the way we live, our needs and desires. But we cannot exist without a meaningful, affective relationship: what inspiration, for example, do we get from 'culture'? What happiness from our way of life?

Mythic expression

Meaning is the realm of myths, which reconcile us to large, impersonal forces and events, over which we have little or no control. Such myths are emotionally charged beliefs that reflect the way in which we experience formative periods in our history. For myths are symbolic representations of reality that from a rational standpoint contain incorrect assumptions; but they are nonetheless authentic, deeply felt responses to social change.

Such are the general conditions of myth-formation, which take on particular forms in any given country, depending on specific historical, social or cultural developments. It is important first to analyse these general conditions in order to provide the basic context from which particular myths arise – such as Le Pen's populist myth of racial superiority, or the elitist myth of national grandeur, or indeed that of French 'exceptionalism': but the last of these, at least, is changing as circumstances change.

Now, these changing conditions – the product in modern times of large-scale capitalism, of power politics, and 'mass' culture – cannot be understood solely from the conventional analysis of a rational mode of production, power-structure and process of socialization. A fuller understanding must take into account belief-systems, including that fusion of concept and emotions by which economic, political and social 'drives' are represented in mythic-cultural forms.

Economic development, pluralist politics and socialization, to repeat, are the everyday expressions of a rational world order. But each dimension has its affective component. 'Capitalism' is not just the rational organization of production, distribution and exchange, or of calculation, profitability and the creation of wealth; it also draws on psychological motivations – rapacity, acquisitiveness, rivalry and selfishness – Nietzschean qualities, the very stuff of myths!

Politics is not just the 'rational choice' of producers and consumers in the electoral market-place, or the articulation and aggregation of interests, resulting in social equilibrium. Politics is the use (and abuse) of power, characterized often by ruthlessness and mendacity, and by the mythic appeal of charismatic leaders.

The search for identity is not simply a matter of social consensus; the identity of a group is also defined in relation to those outside the group – the 'other' – perceived as different from, or hostile to, the group: still another potent source of myths.

To appreciate the significance of such formative conditions indeed requires rational, causal analyses; but such an appreciation also requires a feeling for the inspiration or repulsion aroused by social change. The historian's empathy for his or her subject is an example. So, too, is the interpretation of myths. But it is not only traumatic events that evoke myths. Myths also emerge in response to positive processes: liberal-democratic myths or solidarity-making myths, for example. Critical change is the crucial factor.

Periods of peace and stability, conversely, usually do not evoke myths. Instead, such periods are conducive to the employment of logic and reason: orderly events fit predictable patterns. Nevertheless, because of the fluidity and impermanence of institutions and ideas – consider the impact of current scientific, informational, economic and ecological 'revolutions' – such periods of stability are unlikely to endure. With new crises, new myths appear. The evident alternation of periods of stability and change suggests therefore that there is no historical progression from 'myth' to 'rationality', contrary to Enlightenment expectations. Rather, there is an alternation of phases of mythic expression with periods of rational discourse, corresponding to social disorder and to tranquillity, respectively.

The inspirational character of myths cannot be overlooked. It is this that enables believers to adapt to, and even to shape, the 'reality' of powerful, impersonal forces in society, in these ways: (1) they are able to cope with the existential condition of suffering, which becomes acute in periods of crisis, and thus, by extension, with the problem of evil in the world; (2) they feel they belong to a community ('we' against 'they') providing shelter against present dangers – a community in which their place is recognized; and (3) they are inspired by myth to create a 'good' community, that is, to establish appropriate norms of conduct and the motivation for action to achieve them. Myths, in other words, provide both meaning and identity; these myths are an emotional fulfilment of personality.

Such a debate over reason and emotion can also be considered as a
clash between 'classical' and 'romantic' perspectives: rationality and order
versus intuition and change which, from one point of view, are antithetical.
But from another point of view they are complementary, each making up
for the inadequacy of the other.

As the philosopher, Y. Yovel, explains:

> Reason is neither complete nor transparent. It contains constitutive
> 'impurities' that are impossible to eliminate and it opens the way to a
> plurality of possible interpretations. Contingency, margins of uncer-
> tainty, breaks in communication, as well as the dependence (in part) of
> rational judgment on the unacknowledged: language, desire, will to
> power, etc. These are not 'accidents', which come to disturb the
> 'normal' functioning of reason, but characteristics that one must
> accept – as far as possible reducing their effects – but without
> expecting to eliminate them, nor for that matter despairing of the
> rational project as a whole.
>
> (Interview with Roger-Pol Droit, *Le Monde*, 23 June 1992.
> And see John Girling, *Myths and Politics in Western
> Societies*, especially Introduction and Conclusion)

The importance of the 'unacknowledged' – taking the form of myths –
is particularly striking in a country like France, where elites pride themselves on their superior rationality and on the excellence of 'Cartesian
logic', inherited from the great seventeenth-century philosopher and math-
ematician, René Descartes.

Rational project: French specificity and Cartesian logic?

'The world loves France because, in France, it recognizes Descartes and
those who have followed him.' 'You know to what extent the most clear
and sensitive characteristics of the French spirit are marked by the thought
of this great man.' The first quotation is from the Communist leader,
Maurice Thorez, in 1946! The second is from the poet Paul Valéry, cele-
brating in 1937 the 300th anniversary of Descartes' *Discours de la méthode*.

As François Azouvi points out (*Le Monde*, 29 March 1996), this is a most
unusual, even unprecedented affair: a philosopher who has come to
symbolize a nation, which he is supposed to resemble, a nation which actually defines itself by reference to this philosopher. To be 'Cartesian' is to be
rational, to have the taste for clarity and method: '*Descartes, c'est la France*',
according to the philosopher André Glucksmann in a book with this title!

This was certainly not the way Descartes was seen during his lifetime; nor did anyone in the 'Age of Enlightenment' dream of identifying Descartes with France. The 'creation of a myth', writes Azouvi, was the work of the French Revolution, which viewed the philosopher as one who 'broke the fetters on the human spirit', thus preparing the way for the 'destruction of political slavery'. Thus did a free nation honour a man who furnished the conceptual instruments of its liberation. It was this 'legendary paternity' that played the decisive role in the nineteenth as in the twentieth century of the idea that Descartes was the incarnation of France. In a formula: France = reason = political freedom = Descartes.

Descartes symbolizes French belief in logic: 'the certainty of clear and distinct ideas, of the exigency of method, the bringing to light of logical truths, founded on reason and its proper qualities rather than on authority and tradition', as Roger-Pol Droit puts it (*Le Monde*, 29 March 1996). But this emphasis on logic obscures Descartes' own last project: to understand the mechanism of our emotions. The problem was a difficult one for Descartes, given his 'radical distinction' between body and mind. For the 'enigma' consisted, not in the adjustment of two separate entities, but in their admixture. (We feel love or hatred, joy or sadness, not as physical effects, but as belonging only to the mind.) To pass from metaphysics to morality, treating of the emotions or 'passions', Descartes had to redefine his conception of the moral subject, which no longer derived purely from the mind, but from the composite mind–body. The foundation of Cartesian morality, according to Droit, was thus 'affective generosity' or responsible 'self-love' acting virtuously.

So far, then, from Descartes symbolizing 'logic' as the distinctive characteristic of French thought, as the current myth suggests, the philosopher of the 'passions' could also be considered to be the father of 'latinity', that is, the generous expression of emotions. Indeed, this more complex interpretation of Descartes is suggested in André Robinet's introduction to the *Discours de la méthode*. The most contradictory positions, he explains, have been taken by writers on Descartes. Some consider the *Discours* to be an atheist attack on religion, or the affirmation of a mystic, the abnegation of responsibility or audacity in the reform of mentalities, overly historical or lacking a historical sense, very logical or not at all, either moralistic or unconventional, either seeking subsidies or sublimely disinterested!

Nevertheless, a distinctive personality does seem to emerge from the *Discours*. As Descartes writes in the first part: 'good sense' (*le bon sens*) is shown in

the ability to judge well, to distinguish the true from the false, in a word, this is reason, which is shared among everybody. The diversity of our opinions is not due to the fact that some are more reasonable than others, but because we conduct our thoughts by different channels. It is not enough to have a good mind; it is important to apply it well.

And again:

I very much esteemed eloquence and loved poetry; but I thought they were both intellectual gifts and not the fruits of study. Those who reason most strongly and order their thoughts best, so as to make them clear and intelligible, are the most persuasive in their proposals . . . even if they have never learned rhetoric.

I most enjoyed mathematics, because of the certainty and the evidence of its reasons . . . but I was astonished that so little had been built on such firm and solid foundations.

Yet Descartes quitted his scholastic studies, believing that he would do better by relying on himself, or on the 'great book of the world', by travelling.

For it seemed to me that I could encounter much more truth in the reasoning of people about the things that were important to them – since they would soon be punished as a result if they had judged badly – than in the reasoning of a man of letters in his study, concerning speculations which have no effect and are inconsequential, except for his vanity . . . .I always had the extreme desire to learn to distinguish the true from the false, to see clearly in my actions, and to walk with assurance in this life.

Such an open-minded, practical attitude is surely very different from the mythical Descartes, bearer of abstract logic!

Twin paradox

Now, logic and latinity, to repeat, are code-words for the cognitive and affective approaches to 'reality' – the world we construct for ourselves. The French, as can be seen from the example of Descartes, are no different from anybody else in this respect. The 'French exception', however, is that they are more extreme – both in logic and latinity – than the Anglo-Saxons.

The French (especially the elites) pride themselves on their logic; but their activities, from an Anglo-Saxon standpoint, are often seen as typically 'latin': buoyant, spontaneous, volatile, individualistic, even *indocile* (unmanageable). Yet, whatever the appeal of logic, latinity derives more from social conditions than it does as a national stereotype. (Who said his countrymen were 'ungovernable'? That stolid Anglo-Saxon, Prime Minister Heath.)

Latinity reflects popular fears or suspicions of a hostile or uncertain environment. Hence the reliance, not on political parties or the state (except in the hope of handouts), but on one's family, relatives, friends, associates, 'connections', patrons, and ultimately on oneself. Where 'logic' calls for co-operation with the state and political institutions, for mutual advantage, 'latinity' calls for confrontation, often in the most dramatic fashion. Such examples are the 'events' of 1968 and the waves of strikes against Prime Minister Juppé's 'rational' reforms, in November–December 1995. 'For reasons belonging to our culture,' laments President Chirac (*Le Journal du dimanche*, 26 January 1997), 'the French have a lot of difficulty in accepting reforms. Because we lack a culture of dialogue, reforms are produced sporadically, between long periods of paralysis.'

Hence the 'twin paradox': latinity is individualistic and anarchic, yet it creates a feeling of solidarity when manifested – with drama – in the street; at the same time logic – the rational advocacy of planned, co-operative efforts – founders on doctrinal disputes (as well as personal and factional rivalries) when doctrines are taken to extremes, that is to say to their 'logical conclusion'.

The mass-confrontational aspect of latinity towards logic derives, basically, from reaction to French elitism. The elitist 'system', convinced of its own superiority, intelligence and reason – treating people as if they were units in an industrial blueprint – provokes the resentment of those so treated, thus demonstrating that they are not cogs in a machine, but (unpredictable, even unmanageable) human beings.

The complementary relations of logic and latinity are equally significant. The democratic system, for example, mobilizes popular solidarity (latinity) for a logical purpose: to vote out governments, whose policies are ineffective or unpopular (thus, the defeat of the Left in 1993, of the Right in 1997).

In wartime, too, it is necessary to mobilize solidarity, using all the emotional appeals of latinity, so as to sustain the morale of the 'front': 'unity makes force' is a logical way to oppose the enemy. Similarly, environmental campaigners mobilize popular feelings (embracing the trees) against the logic of industrial 'progress' – but in support of the larger logic of defence of the endangered planet.

Here are further examples of the importance in French life of latinity and logic.

'Disobedience: the natural unmanageability of the French is not a defect', argues François Léotard, president of the UDF (*Le Monde*, 22 February 1997). 'Our national temperament is expressed throughout our history by a taste for revolt, which is generally brought about in response to authoritarian governments.' (Admittedly, Léotard went on to warn that disobedience should not be at the risk of 'our national cohesion'.)

Simone de Beauvoir exemplifies the latinity of rebellion in the streets. It was the period when France was polarized over Algeria: 'the whole country had let itself be convinced that there was only one alternative: de Gaulle or the paras.' To Sartre and Beauvoir this was no choice: both sides, they believed, were intent on pursuing war to the end. De Gaulle declared that he was ready to 'assume the powers of the Republic'. To oppose him, the Communist-led trade union movement (CGT) called for strike action.

Instantly responding, Sartre and Beauvoir took a taxi to a metro stop, where they joined the demonstration.

> We marched behind the banner of the Beaux-Arts to find ourselves behind the 'Droits de l'Homme'. Old Republicans were jubilant, because it made them younger by half a century. They jumped in the air, looking over the heads of the marchers, to see the length of the procession . . . a merry crowd and a wise crowd, which obeyed its orders . . . 'De Gaulle to the museum – the paras to the factory': these slogans had a great success.
>
> (*La Force des choses*, 415–17)

What was astonishing, she recalled, was the vivacity of the crowd. 'But some of us remarked that the people were too good-humoured, they were happy to shout and to sing, but not at all determined on action'; moreover, the strike had failed.

'Direct action is noisy, causes inconvenience and may catch the head-lines', reports an observer, not a participant (Anne Stevens, *The Government and Politics of France*, 305–6). But she believes its success is infrequent. The violence of steelworkers in the late 1970s may have improved redundancy terms but did nothing to halt the restructuring of the industry. Air France's plans to rationalize the ailing network will take effect over a longer period than was envisaged before the strike, but the airline cannot be indefinitely sheltered from the need to adapt to changing conditions. Blocking roads with farm animals, as in 1993, is spectacular but has little effect on the overall trends of the European Common Agricultural Policy. 'Nor should the phenomenon be exaggerated. The numbers of working days lost through strikes declined through the 1980s. Violent direct action, although always newsworthy, is sporadic and isolated.' (Conversely, Wright, *The Government and Politics of France*, 262, gives examples of successful demonstrations, which have resulted in humiliating policy reversals by governments.)

Finally, an example of latinity and failure of logic, from Gary P. Freeman, 'Financial crisis and policy continuity in the Welfare State' (in Hall, Hayward and Machin, eds, *Developments in French Politics*, 188–98). Social spending has increased to well over one-quarter of domestic product, providing about one-third of French family income. But contributions weigh heavily on workers' wages and make up as much as 30 per cent of the cost of labour to business. The ageing of the population and increase in unemployment have resulted in an explosion of costs.

Yet the French social security system, although intended – logically – to be universalistic, is in practice strongly particularistic (subjected to influential pressure groups) operating under a selective tangle of regulations and administrative units. Benefits and the contributions to pay them vary enormously between workers in industry and in agriculture and at different levels of skill. 'Austere, calculated and technocratic in style, social policy is bargained, chaotic and distinctively reactive in substance': logic and latinity, par excellence!

References

Beauvoir, S. de (1963) *La Force des choses*, Paris: Gallimard.

Descartes, R. (1637) *Discours de la méthode*.

Freeman, G. (1994) 'Financial crisis and policy continuity in the Welfare State' in P. Hall, J. Hayward and H. Machin (eds) *Developments in French Politics*, London: Macmillan.

Gaulle, Ch. de (1959) *Mémoires de guerre – L'Appel 1940–1942*, Paris: Plon.

Girling, J. (1993) *Myths and Politics in Western Societies*, New Brunswick, N.J.: Transaction.

Le Monde, various.

Robinet, A. (1969) introduction to R. Descartes, *Discours de la méthode*, Paris: Larousse.

Stevens, A. (1996) *The Government and Politics of France*, London: Macmillan.

Wright, V. (1989) *The Government and Politics of France*, London: Routledge.

11 Culture

Comment resterait-elle l'incomparable représentation de la pensée, de la
langue, de la littérature françaises qu'elle devait être par destination et qui
avait, depuis trois siècles, si puissament contribué au rayonnement de notre
pays?

Charles de Gaulle

Cultural pride is to France as logic is to Descartes. But culture is under
threat, not from latinity (as logic sometimes is), but from two other direc-
tions: from the commercialization of values in a global market economy,
from outside; and from 'postmodernist' relativism, which is partly home
grown.

Just as democratic institutions and civil society work towards the fulfilment of the political dimension of personality, and family life, friendship
and voluntary associations towards the fulfilment of the social, so myth, art
and ritual fulfil the cultural dimension of personality. Culture is the tran-
scendence of the everyday, the creation of imaginary worlds. As for the
economic dimension, few activities – apart from those of inventors and
entrepreneurs – are fulfilling; nevertheless, economic resources are fundamental to all other dimensions.

Culture has been represented as an ordered system of meaning and
symbols in terms of which individuals define their world, express their feelings and make their judgements (quoted by Clifford Geertz, *The
Interpretation of Cultures*, 68). But this is too inclusive. Individuals also 'define
their world', distinctively, in either political or social terms. The 'system of
meaning and symbols', in my view, is common to all three dimensions.
There is, however, as Geertz notes, another division: between intellective
communication by speech and writing, and affective communication, by
cultural symbols and meanings.

Nevertheless, there is an interpenetration of culture, politics and society.
Thus Goethe, speaking of patriotism, asks:

What is meant by love of one's country? What is meant by patriotic deeds? If the poet has employed a life battling with pernicious prejudices, in setting aside narrow views, in enlightening the minds, purifying the tastes, ennobling the feelings and thoughts of his countrymen, what better could he have done? How could he have acted more patriotically?

(Conversations with Eckermann, March 1832)

Descartes, too, exemplifies the blossoming of culture before the 'Age of Reason'. In his *Discours* he commends:

> Languages, which are necessary for understanding ancient books; the ingenious pleasure of fables, which awaken the spirit; the memorable actions in history which, read with discretion, help to form judgement; reading of good books, which is like a conversation with all the cultivated persons of past centuries . . . eloquence, with its incomparable strength and beauty; poetry with its delightful delicacy and sweetness; mathematics, with its subtle inventions, which . . . eases the work of man; writings on customs and morality, which provide very useful exhortations to virtue; theology, which teaches us the way to salvation; philosophy, which gives us the means to speak of the probability of all things . . . jurisprudence, medicine and other sciences, which bring honour and wealth to those who cultivate them; and finally, it is good to have examined all these, even the most superstitious and false, in order to know their true value and to prevent oneself being deceived.

Descartes is the precursor of the Age of Enlightenment. He is far removed from feudal culture, and its obsession with violence and death, its love of honour and pageantry, and faith in loyalty and hierarchy. He is equally far from the materialist culture of the industrial revolution – as he is from the postmodernist culture of post-industrial society.

Surveying this evolution of culture, Raymond Williams, in *Culture and Society 1780–1950*, brings out, appropriately for the 'first industrial nation', the pioneering critiques of Thomas Carlyle, historian of the French Revolution, and Matthew Arnold, the great educational reformer, in the mid-nineteenth century.

'Were we required to characterize this age of ours', writes Carlyle, we should be tempted to call it, not a heroic, devotional, philosophical or moral age, but above all the 'Mechanical Age', where 'all is by rule and calculated contrivance'. The result is the growth of wealth, 'strangely altering the old relations, and increasing the distance between rich and poor'. Not only does the age of machinery affect external circumstances, but the internal and spiritual also:

> The same habit regulates not our modes of action alone, but our modes of thought and feeling . . . .Intellect, the power man has of knowing and believing, is now nearly synonymous with Logic, or the mere power of arranging and communicating . . . .In all senses, we worship and follow after Power.
>
> (quoted by Williams, 86–7)

Matthew Arnold, in *Culture and Anarchy*, also conceives of culture as 'true human perfection', developing all sides of our humanity. But Arnold could find in none of the social classes the quality of culture. The aristocracy (depicted as Barbarians), intent on defending the status quo, were inaccessible to the free play of new ideas. The middle classes (Philistines) were also useless, because their faith in machinery denied the pursuit of individual and social perfection. As for the working classes (Populace) they either tried to ape the material pursuits of the middle classes, or were degraded and brutal, the repository of darkness rather than light.

The means of awakening, for Arnold, were especially education, poetry and criticism. Education sets standards of effective thinking, based on the 'best that has been thought and written in the world'. Poetry sets a standard of beauty and the perfection of human nature. Finally criticism creates, by the free play of intelligence, the 'authority of the best self' (Williams, 124–5, 129–30).

Williams himself formulates the idea of culture as the recognition of a body of moral and intellectual activities that are separate from and an alternative to industrial society. Culture presupposes a new kind of social and personal relations. In this way, the early meaning of culture is joined, and changed, by the growing assertion of a whole way of life, not only as a scale of integrity, but as a mode of interpreting our common experience and, by interpreting, to change it. He concludes that the compatibility of increasing specialization (in the socio-economic world) with a 'genuinely common culture' is only solvable in the context of a material community and by the full democratic process. By this he means effective participation and recognition of the equality of human beings (Williams, 17–18, 318). But how, under present conditions, can a genuinely common culture be achieved?

For culture is not only a process, varying throughout the ages, but it is a state that is divided in itself: between 'high' or elitist culture and 'low' or mass culture. Each of these forms of culture faces a growing threat: from the commercialization of values in a global market economy (especially so with popular culture); and from the relativity, or trivialization, of values in 'postmodern' society (eroding or perverting 'high' or elitist culture).

Cultural relativism

Paradoxically, it is not the strength of postmodernist theorizing – notably 'deconstruction', eclecticism, and the dismissal of transcendent values – but its weakness that is most prejudicial to 'high' culture. For postmodernism invites comparison with that master of deconstruction, Nietzsche, whose 'death of God' leaves a terrifying void – after centuries of habituation to the ideas, feelings and beliefs in a divine presence. History repeats itself, to appropriate Hegel's aphorism, first as tragedy (the Nietzschean void) then as farce (postmodernism).

Postmodernism both reflects and expresses, especially in France, the 'void' in what was once a great, 'universal' culture. Belief in that culture persists. Thus to Prime Minister Jospin, in his 'declaration of general policy' (June 1997),

Culture is the soul of democracy. The works of the mind, the fruits of creation, cannot be assimilated to merchandise or products like any other. Bearers of universal values, cultural works are also the expression of our national and European singularity. The government will be particularly vigilant in the defence of our cultural exception.

These noble sentiments (nobility, like elitism, is derided by postmodernists) were repeated, to the verge of caricature, by a pillar of the establishment, Albert Chambon, ambassador of France. Writing in *Le Figaro* (8 August 1997), he declared that France, ever since the fifth century, 'has become the cradle of a [Catholic] civilization that has become universal'. Undeterred by revolutionary excess, France then moved from bearer of 'Christian spirituality' to that of 'conquering and flamboyant humanism', spreading beyond the frontiers of Europe. No other European people, Chambon insisted, can boast of such a heritage. 'No other European people can, as we can, feel ourselves invested, in the realm of the spirit, with a civilizing mission on such a scale.' But if this country 'with its universal vocation' is condemned to dissolve itself in a 'conglomerate of various peoples', the ambassador warned, then France will no longer have a reason to exist.

Chambon's (exaggerated) contrast between the glory of the past and the ignoble prospects of the future Europe demonstrates precisely the postmodernist void. In a world deprived of God, in a France that has lost its ideological idols (notably Marxism) as well as its artistic hegemony (to the

United States), what else is left but feebleness, uncertainty and indifference to values?

It is surely appropriate in this postmodernist world that the celebrated *Guide Vert Michelin*, reputed for awarding three stars to outstanding areas of natural beauty, of historic importance or cultural renown, should also offer its highest distinction to Disneyland Paris. Indeed, among the Disneyland attractions, Big Thunder Mountain, Phantom Manor and Pirates of the Caribbean all get three stars – along with the Palace of Versailles, the Cathedral of Saint-Denis and Fontainebleau! Does not this say something about the present attrition of cultural values – and the inroads of commercialism?

For postmodernism, reflecting the weakness of present-day 'high' culture and the prevalence of 'low' culture, in its indifference to ascribed values undermines the already fragile defence of 'public service' standards – in broadcasting and the press, for example, which are deemed to be 'elitist' – and thus opens the way for the further encroachment of commercial practices and values.

As the British critic Richard Hoggart points out, in *The Way We Live Now*, 'The wave of relativism – the obsessive avoidance of judgments of quality, or moral judgment – has risen higher than ever before (as in all prosperous societies).' He goes on: 'If no distinction of quality can be made, why should it not be agreed that the one distinction that can be made, the one test, is that of popularity by numbers? So the charts rule.' He concludes,

> Where else is there to go? If you refuse comparative judgments based on a work's perceptiveness, power of language, attempted and to some degree achieved truth and honesty before experience, you have to accept the definitive power of numbers; you are in a world entirely relativist except for head-counting.
>
> (p. 60)

Moreover, the postmodernist privileging of the 'cultural signal', referring to the 'sign' in a universe of signs and not the substance (considered to imply an unacceptable value-judgement), is, as the philosopher Bernard-Henri Lévy puts it, to lump together, with no way to distinguish them, 'a package by [the manufacturer] Saint-Gobain and a page by [the poet] Saint-John Perse'. Think, he goes on, of that improbable find, yet so typical of the epoch, which is the notion of 'creator': the publicity agent, the promotion film-maker, the ready-to-wear stylist and the inheritors of Joyce and Flaubert, all embarked in the same galley, all together in the same concept! (*Eloge des intellectuels*, 16–17).

Indeed, the celebrated theorist of power/knowledge relations in society, Michel Foucault, had himself criticized Jacques Derrida's 'textual deconstruction' for trying to exclude all questions about the truth claims of texts. For Foucault, as for Lévy, there are texts about how people understand themselves and what sort of life they esteem, that is, authenticity (David C. Hoy, *Foucault*, 20). Contrary to the 'passivity' of much postmodernist theorizing, Foucault's own research has been intellectually invigorating: in particular, his investigation of the 'rules of right' in society (sovereignty, the state, obedience) which, he claims, mask the 'effects of truth', namely, the production of 'scientific' knowledge by the dominant culture, conditioning the way people think and thus 'normalizing' their behaviour (Michel Foucault, *Power/Knowledge*, 93–5, 103–5).

In effect, whatever the explanatory power of postmodernist theory (which is weak, reflecting weakness, in my view), its levelling of 'elitist' standards saps resistance to the meretricious (considered no better or worse than anything else), thus opening the way for market forces to take over. 'When the frontier between culture and entertainment is blurred,' as Alain Finkielkraut insists, 'there is no longer a space in which to welcome works of culture or to give a meaning to them' (*La défaite de la pensée*, 158).

Thus, in the postmodern era of the 'dissolution of the social', according to Alain Touraine, there is no other way to regulate society except by tolerance. He quotes Gilles Lipovetsky's *L'Ere du vide*: 'All forms of taste or behaviour can coexist without excluding one another, everything can be chosen at leisure, the simple life as well as the hyper-sophisticated one, in a devitalized time without parameters or stable definitions.'

In Touraine's view, the postmodernist movement 'rejects the functional differentiation of the realms of social life – art, economics, politics – and their complement, the everyday use of instrumental reason'. Similarly, it refuses any separation between social, political or aesthetic high culture and mass culture. Indeed, for Fredric Jameson, postmodern culture is defined by pastiche and schizophrenia: pastiche, because the postulated absence of unity in a culture leads to eclectic reproduction of past styles; and schizophrenia, because enclosure in a 'perpetual present' suppresses the space which would allow unity of culture to be created (Touraine, *Critique de la modernité*, 242–3, 246–7).

Fragmented society, undifferentiated values and loss of historical reference, on the one hand, and society united by reason, transcendent values (distinguishing between high and low culture) and sense of historical development, on the other: is there no middle way between the dissolution suggested by the postmodern and the archaism of the conventional or the traditional?

Let us consider this question from the standpoint of three related issues:

the projection of (French) civilization; human rights; and the autonomous subject.

First, the 'civilizing mission': the watchwords of the French Revolution – liberty, equality and fraternity – were undoubtedly charged with a sense of universality; liberty was not just for the French people who had over-thrown feudal despotism and the power of the privileged, but for all those in Europe who were fighting for a similar cause and, in principle, for everyone throughout the world. Similarly, all should be equal under the law and with equal political rights. This condition marks the fraternity of all people engaged in the struggle for 'natural rights': life, liberty, security and property. All these, in turn, became France's *mission civilisatrice*: to enlighten the benighted natives of the French colonial empire. Asian and African children did imbibe these high principles at school; but when they graduated it was another story.

Human rights, endorsed by the United Nations, present a similar problem. Human rights are universal or they are nothing. Yet a number of UN member countries either claim that human rights are a Western impo-sition (in effect, cultural imperialism) or that 'Asian values' – or, more generally, 'Third World' values – are more appropriate to their peoples. According to these regimes, their cultures are different from those in the West. (Consider, in this respect, the cynical comments by President Mitterrand on the killings in Rwanda, reported in *Le Figaro*, 12 January 1998: 'In countries like that, genocide is not so important.') In reality, it is not so much that cultures differ, but that power-structures differ. As in war, human rights are among the first casualties of authoritarian rule; any attempt to protect individuals (especially critical individuals) against abuse poses a direct threat to the power of the abuser.

Human rights, contrary to postmodernist theorizing, thus represent transcendent values; contrary to traditional practice, their enforcement requires a 'universal' struggle.

Finally, the autonomous subject: the 'essential' dignity of the individual human being, as stipulated by the United Nations. Yet the individual as independent actor, fully responsible for his or her utterances and behaviour, is of course a myth. Those 'masters of suspicion' (Paul Ricoeur), Marx and Freud, have undermined the notion of an autonomous subject. For Marx, individuals are defined by their relation to the mode of production and socially by their class; they may believe that they behave independently and speak freely, but that is 'false conscious-ness': they cannot speak or act outside their class position. Even more subversive of autonomy is Freud's insistence on the repressive power of the 'unconscious' mind, conditioning conscious behaviour.

Alain Touraine (and I share his view) takes up a mid-position between economic and psychological determinism and the Enlightenment project of the free (and rational) individual. As he puts it (*Critique de la modernité*, 280–1, 300, 311), the fragmented realm of modernity can only be reunified by the complementary (and contradictory) relations of reason and the subject. For Touraine, the individual subject is socially constructed as an 'actor': an actor, struggling for freedom, in 'social movements' that contest the 'logic of order': that is, the repressive potential or practice of the state and the economy. Instrumental rationality without the subject leads to scientific or technocratic despotism; the subject without rationality leads to anarchy. The subject is not determined, but as an actor has the capacity to change society. Now, cultural activities form an important part of that capacity. For, as Raymond Williams affirms, culture is a means of interpreting society and, by interpreting, to change it.

Commercialized values

Generations of children and adults, as Jean-Michel Djian puts it, are culturally 'fabricated' with and by television and the other media. There is no ideological resistance, he writes, to their irresistible progression. Television, in particular, does not lead to debate, but avoids it. Television gives the illusion of understanding the world, while it only regards it. Nevertheless, television has the potential, above all, to transmit knowledge, understanding and creation.

The gap between the cultural possibilities of television and commercial realities is the underlying theme of the contributors to a special issue (September 1997) of *Le Monde de l'Education*, edited by Dominique Wolton. For the latter, television programmes are 'far from fulfilling the cultural and educational objectives worthy of a modern democracy'. It is one of the greatest challenges of the next century. For the more the spread of television, 'the more one must be vigilant, critical and ambitious in seeing that it remains faithful to its values'.

What are these values? Essentially, the 'popular legitimacy' of television lies in 'creating a link among the millions of people, who all exist separately, in an individual, hierarchical and mass society'. For television is a formidable means of communication, the only one that transcends age, social class and way of life. Now this legitimacy, weak since the beginning of television, is more than ever threatened by the domination of private television over the public channels and the virtual abandonment of the latter to market forces.

Wolton's critique is strikingly endorsed by Richard Hoggart in *The Way We Live Now*. Public service broadcasting (in Britain) is defined in universal terms; and so is its 'betrayal': the title of Hoggart's chapter. Hoggart, a highly respected social critic, is writing of British experience, but his 'message' is relevant to other countries. For if the forms of public broadcasting vary, the threat to high standards – by commercialization of values and by trivialization – is the same everywhere. The principles of public service broadcasting are well worth defining (Hoggart, 114, 119–20):

1   geographic universality – programmes available to the whole population;
2   universal appeal – to cater for the widest possible range of interests and tastes;
3   particular attention to minorities – we are all members of some minority group;
4   national identity – relating to the sense of identity and community;
5   no vested interests – resisting economic or political pressures;
6   direct funding by the users; and
7   encouragement of 'competition in good programming rather than competition for numbers'.

This British 'model' – and subsequent practice – have been replicated throughout the world, and no less in France. Indeed, a historian of French television, Isabelle Veyrat-Masson, notes the enthusiasm of the postwar years, when the country saw the future in terms of popular culture: 'Jean Vilar and the TNP [Théâtre National Populaire], then, later, André Malraux's houses of culture – supreme achievement of that impulse of the Resistance . . . .Did not the small screen appear as the instrument of the great national design to allow access to culture to everyone?' But the promise was not upheld: 'the initial project betrayed' (*Le Monde de l'Education*, September 1997).

For France, as for Britain, the age of creative independence is over. Claude Santinelli, television producer, reports:

Under [President] Giscard, the monopoly of the workers and makers of TV spectacles comes to an end. But the real change is with the arrival of Léotard [as the minister responsible]. Popular television, which for me prolongs the school of Jules Ferry [the great education minister of the Third Republic], disappears behind commercial liberalism and multiplication of channels. The 'programme', that is to say, the human, moral and artistic contract between the people and their television, is dead. And the monster TF1 [the major commercial channel] gradually gains the public sector, which is constrained to imitate the giant.

(*Le Monde de l'Education*, September 1997)

In this way, cultural values are replaced by market values. And of these, the most powerful are the creation of American enterprises, sweeping all before them, leaving European producers the choice of a small protected niche or the derisory imitation of Hollywood. The battle of giant American conglomerates (resulting from the 'megafusions' of 1995) becomes a crucial matter of content. In order 'to keep subscribers faithful or to conquer a new audience', writes Nicole Vulser, 'they concentrate on sporting rights and films'.

Television has become globalized, acknowledges the BBC editor, Nicholas Fraser (*Guardian weekly*, 22 June 1997): 'its familiar forms have been first exported and then copied throughout the world. There is a world media culture now and it consists predominantly of reach-me-down Americana – takings from the great home mass media swamp.' For the new giant corporations are 'not in the business of doing good deeds, or preserving what remains of our public, national cultures':

> In return the new giants do offer distraction. They are professionally concerned with the nature of our private acts of consumption. Since the satellite revolution . . . we have witnessed a huge culture shift. We now have a global market, in which everything can be sold. Information, like entertainment, has become a commodity – but so have television journalists, whose practice, whatever they like to think, is now best understood as an extension of showbusiness . . . .But the most dramatic shift in attitude concerns the current willingness to concede that 'quality' is for rich people and trash is for the masses.

By now the era of 'Homeric battles' to defend the integrity of European programmes against the American tidal wave is long past, confirms Nicole Vulser (*Le Monde*, 4 September 1997). Even if the European Union's 1989 directive permits the creation of quotas for European works, few countries apply them. According to European statistics, in 1995 American companies earned 6.8 billion dollars from sales of programmes on the European market, while European firms exported only 532 million dollars' worth to the United States. As much as 43 per cent of American earnings in 1996 came from exports, up from 30 per cent ten years earlier.

Even in France, champion of the 'cultural exception', American films in March 1997 gained nearly half the market among viewers under fifty of films on TF1, compared with less than a third of the market for French films (Guy Dutheil, *Le Monde*, 13 May 1997). Similarly, for the cinema, American films dominate the market (54 per cent in 1995) compared to French films (37.5 per cent).

As the American scriptwriter William Goldman observed (*Le Monde*, 22 May 1997), ever since *Jaws* made such money in record time, Hollywood constantly seeks to repeat the experience: 'the studios are so obsessed with special effects and violence, and so preoccupied with their business interests in Asia and Europe that they end up making totally stupid films' – although some independent productions are interesting.

Finally, for the 'consumer society' enamoured of American films – and their French copies – *publicité* (advertising) has become a major ingredient, shaping people's tastes, especially among the young, and providing an essential source of funds (and therefore an insidious form of control) in regard to commercial and even 'public' television.

The advertisers, note the historians Serge Berstein and Jean-Pierre Rioux, no longer transmit information: 'They fabricate messages with a suppleness and creativity that overcome all obstacles and pervade all fields: . . . politics itself enters into the game.' The long march towards the promised land of generalized satisfaction has begun: no depth of consumption and peaceful enjoyment is possible without a strategy of desire. Studies of motivation and marketing, originating in the United States, show that people buy and make use of symbols as much as prod-ucts. For television has the immense power to multiply models and signs, producing a mass market for fashions and practices (*La France de l'expansion*, vol. 2, 208–9).

Publicité has become a way of life, or rather a means of survival, for the major television channels. Advertising on television (some 95 per cent of the French population has a TV set) amounted in 1996 to nearly 36 per cent of total media advertising, compared to nearly 40 per cent for the press, and 12 per cent each for posters and radio. In that year the television channels gained some 22 billion francs from advertising, a 7.6 per cent increase on the year before. More than half the total income went to TF1.

Because of budgetary restraints and refusal to increase the licence fee (for political reasons) the main public channel, France 2, now receives half its funds from advertising. 'It is therefore obliged to increase its audience,' concludes Yves-Marie Labé, 'to the probable detriment of its programmes' (*Le Monde de l'Education*, September 1997).

Convergent culture

Culture considered as entertainment and as 'generalized satisfaction' are characteristic features of the middle class, whose values are now prevalent in society. The dissolution of the two historic antagonists, the industrial bourgeoisie and the working class, writes Eugenio Scalfari, leaves middle-class standards as the social norm. Indeed, the 'end of ideology' is reflected in the attitudes of the middle class, where 'everything resembles itself, everything is anonymous . . . where customs, fashions and leisure tend to be equal and pragmatism is the rule'. It is precisely in such a society that television becomes the unifying element (E. Scalfari, editor of *La Repubblica*, in *Le Monde*, 14 October 1994).

Countries where the middle class predominates form a world where, historically, the United States has led the way. For American society, from the earliest days of settlement, has never been dominated by an aristocracy, unlike the countries of Europe. (The plantation owners, although important in the South, were rendered powerless by their defeat in the Civil War.) The immigrant workers, on the other hand, came to assimilate the values of the 'New World', and aspired to middle-class status. Internationally, the middle-class values of the American media are powerfully projected as a result of America's strategic and economic hegemony. The United States is a cultural model (both 'high' and 'low') to which other countries are increasingly drawn.

Television, affective rather than intellective, is emblematic of middle-class (and popular) culture. Guy Debord, author in the late 1960s of *La Société du spectacle*, twenty-five years later analyses the impact of the media on European society and politics. He emphasizes the blurred fluidity of images (contrary to the clarity of ideas) appropriate to a society, where 'for the first time in contemporary Europe, no political party, or even fraction of a party, tries any longer to claim to change anything important'. In the 'society of spectacle', he argues, the disquieting conception that a society can be criticized and changed – prevalent for more than two centuries – exists no more. The absence of reformist or revolutionary criticism, he insists, is not because of the appearance of new arguments, but simply because arguments are now useless (Debord, *Commentaires sur la société du spectacle*, 37). 'Culture is at the expense of conviction,' as Jacques Julliard puts it, 'transforming entertainment into a social function' ('The journey to the centre', in Furet, Julliard and Rosanvallon, *La République du Centre*, 118).

Debord's Orwellian exposure of present-day society (exaggerated though it often is in his work) offers a penetrating critique of the dominance of the 'spectacle', via the media, in the service of the global market economy. This, surely, is a dissident view which itself suggests that criticism is not entirely absent. Nevertheless, the evidence of social conformity and passivity induced by the spectacle bears out Feuerbach's comment (quoted by Debord) that people prefer 'the image to the thing, the copy to the original, the representation to the reality'.

Again in the footsteps of Orwell, Debord asserts that the disappearance of historical knowledge is the first effect of 'domination by the spectacle'. He quotes the naive admiration of a former French president for life in 'a world without memory, where, as if on the surface of the water, image incessantly chases image'. For Debord, however, the world of images is sinister and not charming. For it is created and chosen by someone other than the viewer. As a result, the image constructed by another forms the chief relationship between the individual and the world, which previously the individual had seen for himself or herself: 'the flow of images bears everything in its course, and someone other than the individual governs the simplified depiction of the empirical world . . . allowing no time for reflection' (*Commentaires sur la société du spectacle*, 45) in a perpetual present.

The immediacy and transience of the image, in contrast to the logic of ideas, is reflected in the politics of spectacle. In the absence of ideological antagonism, the medium now shapes the message. Thus, in François Furet's caustic comment (*Le Débat*, no. 26, Sept.–Oct. 1997), France presents above all 'the spectacle of a political scene invaded by demagogy'. The great problems determining the future of the country can only be approached obliquely, avoiding painful solutions. The construction of Europe, for example, is too complex and explosive to provide a good electoral issue and is therefore left in the hands of the elite. Unemployment, in turn, while acknowledged by both Left and Right to be an essential element of the present crisis, cannot be treated realistically (to do so requires reduced labour costs, which would upset the 'acquired assets' of workers and unions) and so the political parties offer false solutions: the 700,000 jobs painlessly proposed by the Left, while the Right operates in a vacuum. The 'strange emptiness' of political debate, according to Pierre Rosanvallon, makes Centrist politics more and more disconnected from social life. Social mobilization is reduced to transient issues, intellectual argument is at its lowest level, passions are exhausted and the imagination is asleep ('Malaise in representation' in Furet, Julliard and Rosanvallon, *La République du Centre*, 136, 139–41).

The politics of avoidance of troublesome issues, in order to assure a state of 'generalized satisfaction' among the public, is typical of advertising strategies. These strategies, in turn, reflect the penetration of economic interests into non-economic (political and social) spheres. The inescapable result is the encroachment of 'low' culture on the standards of 'high' culture, the priority of immediate enjoyment over long-term perspectives, the privileging of appearance instead of substance, emotional gratification rather than intellectual achievement, passivity rather than active engagement.

Consumerism even invades the world of publishing, once considered the stronghold of French cultural expression. Accordingly, profit margins must be enlarged, the variety of production (including scholarly works) must be reduced, and market indicators obeyed. As noted in *Le Monde des livres* (8 August 1997), people brought in from outside the publishing profession – as with other spheres of communication – aim to make bookselling as profitable as are magazines, cable television and the cinema. Moreover, the huge advances paid to authors of bestsellers inevitably detract from the funds available to produce works of quality. The very 'civilization of reading' is threatened by these trends, warns Pierre Nora (*Le Monde*, 18 April 1997). He laments the glory of the recent past when authors like Foucault, Lévi-Strauss, Raymond Aron, Duby and Dumézil opened up 'continents of culture, revealed new fields of knowledge, devoted their time to new and important topics'. Now, these 'twenty glorious years of the human sciences are behind us, and the figures are there to prove it'. A scholarly work, once selling 4,000 or 5,000 copies, for example, now sells 2,000 or fewer than 1,000, with difficulty. Entire academic disciplines are sacrificed to market forces: linguistics is finished; sociology, 'apart from the Bourdieu phenomenon', can hardly be touched; economics has become too specialized; and even literary criticism, 'the former pillar of French culture', is abandoned to specialist publishers who can survive on small editions. Nor are intellectuals spared. Thus, the conflict over intellectual 'engagement' (Sartre) or detachment (Aron) degenerated into a 'ritualistic assertion rather than rational argument', breeding a tendency towards abstraction and self-congratulation (S. Hazareesingh, *Political Traditions in Modern France*, 58–9). Hence the decline of intellectual influence on public life.

Here, too, as in economics and politics, the French 'exception' gives way to global convergence. The 'cultural landmark' is replaced by the 'media swamp' of entertainment, sensationalism and triviality. Popular culture of this kind, exemplified in the enormous sales of 'scandal' or 'people' magazines – in France as elsewhere in the world – is not distinct from dominant middle-class values, but merely an extension of these values. For example, even reputable photographic agencies, such as Gamma, Sigma and Sipa in France, no longer depend on news and other forms of information, but to survive must sell photos of showbiz or other personalities. In the case of Gamma, 40 per cent of its business is now 'personalities', while news photographs, once its staple product, have virtually disappeared due to the lack of interest in them shown by mass-selling magazines (Michel Guerrin, *Le Monde*, 12 September 1997).

Sensational magazines respond to the 'insatiable voyeurism' of the public, writes Albert du Roy in *Le Carnaval des hypocrites* (reviewed by Robert Solé, *Le Monde*, 18 July 1997). 'Stars chase publicity, magazines chase the public, and the public chases the stars.' But the political class and the intellectuals, he insists, are no less affected by the virus of publicity. Indeed, the culture of modernity (versus tradition), in Julliard's words, replaces the old cleavage between Left and Right. Thus, politics itself, according to Rosanvallon, is no longer central to intervention and initiative (*La République du Centre*, 118, 144).

It is no surprise, then, to learn the reaction of the younger generation in France: nearly half (43 per cent), according to a recent poll, consider politics to be essentially the 'management of interests' rather than, as is ostensibly the case, the defence of values (only 8 per cent), or the improvement of everyday life (12 per cent), or to bring about change in society (14 per cent). Conversely, the overwhelming majority (90 per cent) of those aged 20 to 34 state their preference for sporting activities or membership in local associations. Nevertheless, two-thirds appreciate the work of trade unions, but less than half (45 per cent) are satisfied with political parties and 43 per cent with the role of religious movements (Gérard Courtois, *Le Monde*, 18 October 1996).

Popular culture thrives in an environment of group activities – but they are social rather than political. For eight out of ten (from the previous poll), belonging to a group is either a way of making friends or a form of entertainment. Pop music has become the universal symbol of the culture of 'distraction'. The internationally known British band Oasis, for example, is described (in the serious *Guardian weekly*, 24 August 1997) as honing to perfection Oasis trademarks: 'the idiotically catchy hooklines, often brazenly drawing on the Beatles; Liam Gallagher's raw vocals, a reminder of what rock is supposed to be about; the clumsy lyrics that for all their faults still burn into the subconscious'. 'Definitely Maybe' was Oasis at its 'yob-rockin'est', 'All Around the World' is 'monolithic in feel, the guitars screaming up front, bass and drums laying down a stomping foundation, Liam in full mad-for-it mode', This comment may seem embarrassingly hype, but it is a true reflection of the generational divide between 'high' and 'low' culture. Pop culture is a world apart from the traditional (elitist) culture, as this example shows.

In France, too, the 'spread of mass culture' through pop songs and pulp magazines, along with the installation of supermarkets and hypermarkets, has transformed the popular lifestyle. Above all, the expression of hedonistic values, such as the appearance in the 1960s of nude pictures in magazines and cinemas (calling into question the centuries-old tradition of 'decency'), has expanded throughout society (Henri Mendras and Alistair Cole, *Social Change in Modern France*, 8).

Consumer habits reflect the same 'permissive' culture: 'The rejection of duty, of sacrifice, in order to seek pleasure for pleasure's sake, to feel good about oneself (hedonism), combined with the desire for novelty and social differentiation result in shopping becoming a leisure activity where impulse buying is paramount', writes a specialist on advertising and marketing in

France, Eve Gilliard-Russell (Gilliard-Russell, 'A market of 58 million consumers' in S. Perry (ed.), *Aspects of Contemporary France*, 232). Such a mass culture, 'easily consumed', juvenile and no longer belonging to any particular country, still manages to preserve a 'very diluted national sensitivity' which all ages can share (Berstein and Rioux, *La France de l'expansion*, 272). Nevertheless, it is important, in conclusion, not to decry popular 'distraction', but rather to find a means of bridging the cultural divide. 'High' culture is worth achieving, for it aims at intellectual as well as emotional fulfilment: intellectual, because it requires (self) discipline, experience, a life of learning. Unlike social status, moreover, there are no barriers to the attainment of high culture in music, literature, the arts. High culture is pluralist, not elitist. There is no monopoly: in principle it is available to all who desire it.

The twin obstacles to the attainment of such culture are from within (the paralysing relativism and pervasive trivialization of standards) and from without (the penetration of market values). Now, just as there is a legitimate role for the state to ensure the conditions of free and fair economic competition (recognized even by neo-liberals), there is a no less legitimate role for the state – through political engagement and funding – to ensure the conditions of access to a culture that transcends the everyday and reveals new worlds of the imagination.

References

Arnold, M. (1869) *Culture and Anarchy*.
Berstein, S. and Rioux, J.-P. (1995) *La France de l'expansion*, vol. 2, Paris: Seuil.
Debord, G. (1967) *La Société du spectacle*, Paris: Gallimard.
——(1992) *Commentaires sur la société du spectacle*, Paris: Gallimard.
Descartes, R. (1637) *Discours de la méthode*.
Le Figaro, 8 August 1997.
Finkielkraut, A. (1987) *La défaite de la pensée*, Paris: Gallimard.
Foucault, M. (1980) *Power/Knowledge*, ed. C. Gordon, New York: Pantheon.
Fraser, N. (1997) in *Guardian weekly*, 22 June.
Furet, F. (1988) 'La France unie . . . ' in F. Furet, J. Julliard and P. Rosanvallon, *La République du Centre*, Paris: Calmann-Lévy.
——(1997) in *Le Débat*, no. 26, September–October.
Geertz, C. (1973) *The Interpretation of Cultures*, New York: Basic Books.
Gilliard-Russell, E. (1997) 'A market of 58 million consumers' in S. Perry (ed.) *Aspects of Contemporary France*, London: Routledge.
Goethe, J. (1901) *Conversations with Eckermann*, New York: Dunne.
Guardian weekly, 24 August 1997.
Guide Vert Michelin: Ile de France (1991).

Hazareesingh, S. (1994) *Political Traditions in Modern France*, Oxford: Oxford University Press.

Hoggart, R. (1993) *The Way We Live Now*, London: Pimlico.

Hoy, D.C. (1986) *Foucault: A Critical Reader*, London: Blackwell.

Julliard, J. (1988) 'La course au centre' in F. Furet, J. Julliard and P. Rosanvallon, *La République du Centre*, Paris: Calmann-Lévy.

Lévy, B.-H. (1987) *Eloge des intellectuels*, Paris: Grasset.

Lipovetsky, G. (1983) *L'Ere du vide*, Paris: Gallimard.

Mendras, H. and Cole, A. (1991) *Social Change in Modern France*, Cambridge, UK: Cambridge University Press.

Le Monde, various.

Le Monde de l'Education, September 1997.

Le Monde des livres.

Ricoeur, P. (1981) in J. Thompson (ed.) *Hermeneutics and the Critical Sciences*, Cambridge, UK: Cambridge University Press.

Rosanvallon, P. (1988) 'Malaise dans la représentation' in F. Furet, J. Julliard and P. Rosanvallon, *La République du Centre*, Paris: Calmann-Lévy.

Roy, A. du (1997) *Le Carnaval des hypocrites*, Paris: Seuil.

Touraine, A. (1992) *Critique de la modernité*, Paris: Fayard.

Williams, R. (1963) *Culture and Society 1780–1950*, Harmondsworth: Penguin.

12 Identity: society and nation

Comme tout le monde, je constate que, de nos jours, le machinisme
domine l'univers. De là s'élève le grand débat du siècle ....De là sont
sortis, hier, les vastes mouvements: socialisme, communisme, fascisme ....
De là résulte cette évidence que le flot des passions, d'espoirs, de
douleurs ... l'immense brassage humain auquel ils se trouvent soumis ...
placent la question sociale au premier rang de toutes celles qu'ont à
résoudre les pouvoirs publics. Je suis sûr que, sans des changements
profonds et rapides dans ce domaine, il n'y aura pas d'ordre qui tienne.

Charles de Gaulle

'The social question'

Social identity is a sense of belonging – to gender, generation (young, old,
middle-aged), workplace, family, neighbourhood, leisure associations, religion (for some) and politics. These are overlapping definitions. Consider,
for example, young men or women, who may be married, divorced or
living together, with or without children, perhaps unemployed or working
part-time, enjoying variety shows on the television, watching football or
earning enough to go on holidays in exotic places, and voting for the
Socialists, the Greens or the RPR. In other words, each individual
constructs from a combination of particular or local activities a social identity, for himself or herself, which is not fixed but varies according to time
and place.

There are also overarching definitions: the sense of belonging to a
nation, to a democratic country, to a system of social welfare (providing
unemployment allowances or old age pensions) and as consumer or
producer within the capitalist system.

National identity, above all, provides a strongly emotional sense of
conformity to particular values, traditions and beliefs, often defined in
contrast to the 'other', whether a 'foreign' country or a 'stranger' within.

This sense of conformity is especially evident in countries like the United States, making for the assimilation of American values among disparate masses of immigrants; and also Japan, as a result of the need both to identify with China – the source of civilization – and to assert Japan's distinctive history and culture, and therefore its independence. These strong psychological pressures are in contrast to the more relaxed attitudes of settled European societies, allowing for a greater variety of 'unthreatening' behaviour – except in times of war and internal crisis!

In the second place, there is social identity, the sense of belonging to a particular society. Such a society is substantially defined by its system of social welfare, or rather the social attitudes that underpin that system. Basically, the individual citizen either has a stake in the society that 'cares' for him or her and provides a safety net in case of misfortune, or else lives in a 'minimum' society of neo-liberal prescription, affirming self-reliance rather than welfare 'dependence', achievement rather than 'entitlement' and individualism rather than membership of a community. The degree of social welfare, in other words, significantly defines the kind of society in which people live.

Democracy, in turn, defines the way in which citizens perceive society and the state. The theoretical equality of political decisions (electing the 'people's representatives') presumes the equal worth of every individual regardless of economic or social differences. In practice, however, economic inequality tends to override political equality. Currently, the logic of economic survival in an increasingly competitive world dominates political life to the detriment of the democratic conception of the 'common good' to which ordinary people aspire.

Finally, and consequently, capitalism structures the individual, whether as consumer or producer, worker or executive, the 'excluded' or the shareholder. Early capitalism ferociously divided society between proletariat and bourgeoisie. By the mid-twentieth century, however, a series of remarkable social and economic changes, such as the 'managerial revolution', the rise of the service sector and the growing importance of information technology, on the one hand, and the countervailing power (to a certain extent) of trade unions and the welfare state, on the other, have moderated these 'primitive' economic antagonisms. The result is the blurring of ideological-political divisions, ushering in the broadly accepted 'norms', throughout society, of the middle class. Whatever the occupational category, a majority considers itself 'middle class' – as much as 58 per cent even of workers and farmers – according to the political studies survey by Cevipof in 1997 (*Le Monde économie*, 23 December 1997).

In this chapter, I discuss 'social identity' in greater detail: economic distribution (rich and poor, jobs and unemployment, 'exclusion'); insecurity and the fragmented society; but also movements of solidarity. I conclude with 'national identity': notably the controversial issue of immigration, exploited above all by the extreme-Right, and the crucial role of France within Europe.

Social identity

Rich and poor

In his inaugural speech in June 1997, Prime Minister Jospin declared:

> There is something in our society that is as absurd as it is unjust. Altogether, we have never been so rich, and yet thousands of people sleep in the street, others cannot look after themselves properly because of lack of money, and there are children who cannot even go to their school canteens. Fear of the future is stronger than ever . . . . To find a place in society is first of all to have a job.

For losing a job is often the first step in a chain of events that leads to the deprivation or homelessness of an individual or an entire family, reported Xavier Emanuelli, secretary of state for humanitarian action in the Juppé government. Writing in *Le Monde* (15 April 1997), he estimated that two million people were poorly housed in France and 100,000 to 200,000 lived in the street. The result is 'exclusion': 'separation from a whole network of affective and social exchanges, a loss of bearings, an incapacity to project themselves into the future . . . inability to express their rights or undertake their responsibilities'. The resulting poverty and deprivation should be unacceptable for a rich nation.

European Community statistics for 1993 (*Le Monde*, 18–19 May 1997) showed 14 per cent of French people living in poverty, defined as earning less than half the average income, compared to 11 per cent in Germany – but 22 per cent in Britain. Unemployment contributed a great deal to such deprivation; but a third of poor households were at work. The single-parent family, with children under 16, was most at risk, followed by isolated young people under 30, and then retired people over 65, living on their own.

The 1997 survey by the charity Secours catholique of households in the previous year revealed three-quarters of a million 'poverty situations' – a 10 per cent increase on the year before – and a record figure for the past sixteen years. The total numbers living in poverty amount to some two million people, half of them children (Jérôme Fenoglio, *Le Monde*, 6 November 1997).

At the other end of the scale, the richest households – 1 per cent of the total – owned one-fifth of the national wealth (National Institute for Statistical and Economic Studies, Insee: *Le Monde*, 25 September 1997). In terms of housing, the rich owned 5 per cent of the total; they also owned nearly 40 per cent of stocks and shares. According to Insee's September 1996 study (referring to 1992 figures) the poorest 25 per cent of households, by contrast, owned only 1 per cent of the total wealth; and even half the households owned only 8 per cent. The richest 5 per cent of households, on the other hand, owned nearly 40 per cent of national wealth.

The rich in France are exceptionally wealthy. Another French 'exception' is the character and size of unemployment. This has grown like a disease in recent years. In the mid-1970s, unemployment was below 3 per cent. It had doubled by the end of the decade, and nearly doubled again (to 10 per cent) in the mid-1980s, reaching 12 per cent a decade later. It is particularly unfortunate, writes Michel Godet, a specialist on employment (*Le Monde*, 9 September 1997), that France has among the highest rates of unemployment for young people between 16 and 25 years old. Admittedly, more now remain in school or university. But under one in three is economically active.

Altogether, in June 1997, there were some three million unemployed; more than one-third were 'long-term', that is, unemployed for more than one year. From statistics of the Centre for Health and Social Protection, Credes (*Le Monde*, 4 June 1997), more than half of those seeking work were women. Significantly, the less educated formed the great majority of those looking for jobs. Although the unemployed were more likely to be ill than those at work, only 57 per cent of them had complementary medical assurance compared to 84 per cent of those at work. (The range of measures to deal with unemployment – and their cost – is detailed in Alain Gubian's article in *L'Etat de la France 97–98*; see also articles by P.-A. Audirac and Carla Saglietti in the same work, 448–61.)

The standard of living of unemployed households could be estimated as 30 to 40 per cent lower than for those at work (Insee statistics: Philippe Baverel, *Le Monde*, 3 September 1997). Although the average consumption of unemployed families was some 22 per cent below that of the employed (222,000 francs in 1995), the deficit nearly doubled for the long-term unemployed. Even gloomier conclusions were drawn by the Planning Commission (commissariat général du Plan), reported in *Le Monde* of 3 September 1997, which indicated that nearly 7 million people were directly or indirectly affected by unemployment, including those with short-term jobs. The report confirmed the 'growing insecurity', indebtedness, and psychological consequences of unemployment.

Insecurity

The 'social fracture', denounced by Jacques Chirac during his successful presidential campaign in 1995 (but later forgotten), remained unchanged for nearly half the people polled in April 1997. A slightly smaller proportion (44 per cent) believed it had got worse. 'Social fracture' appropriately defines the division between rich and poor, the high rate of unemployment, particularly among the young, and persistent 'exclusion' from society of the poor, the homeless and minorities.

As Michel Rocard, the former Socialist prime minister, points out (*Le Monde*, 19 June 1997), besides 3.5 million unemployed, there are more than 4 million people in precarious jobs, especially short-term (often less than two months) or state-supported. The negative social consequences, he writes, are evident: 'lack of qualifications, alcoholism, drugs, breaking-up of families and delinquency'.

A Credoc report (Centre for Research and Documentation on Living Conditions) shows that major French preoccupations in February 1997 were unemployment, serious illness, poverty in France, drugs and worldwide poverty. But other studies reveal the significance of 'insecurity', especially in 'sensitive' areas, such as the working-class suburbs of major cities. Here 'insecurity' reflects localized criminality as well as 'anti-social behaviour', where broken windows are not replaced and stolen vehicles are not recovered (Erich Inciyan, *Le Monde*, 26 February 1997). Protests against insecurity are emphasized in the platform of the National Front, with the implication that the established political parties are unable or unwilling to do much to help ordinary people in their everyday life.

Children involved in anti-social behaviour, according to a study by *Le Monde* (29 July 1997), generally come from broken homes or one-parent families. These families live from day to day, said one teacher. 'It is difficult to tell them that their six-year-old should not be out on the streets at night, not because it is really dangerous, but because when the child is twelve it will be hard to make that boy or girl understand that there have to be some rules.' Yet, as a judge of a children's court noted, children in trouble are often 'left to themselves because their parents are not interested in them; they know no limits'. A social worker, however, referred to more serious cases: 'Those problem-children are often used by those who are older to help them in illegal activities, such as carrying small packets of narcotics, watching out [for police], burning cars.' They all agreed that ways to prevent juvenile delinquency run up against the same limits – the lack of funds.

Violence in schools is symptomatic. Schools in some areas, founded to educate children as future citizens, have turned out to be centres of bullying and aggression, even against teachers. The sociologist Christian Bachman, interviewed by *Le Monde* (24 May 1997), argued that the problem was not just a matter of individuals, but of a whole 'street culture' that had taken over as a result of the disappearance during the last twenty years of 'socially integrating' factors. Indeed, violent behaviour was affecting ever-younger children. A growing number were even going to prison. Nearly half the *lycées* and colleges, according to school inspectors (*Le Figaro*, 15 September 1997), were affected by violence, and as many as 81 per cent of those in the suburbs of Paris. An earlier survey of school children (*Le Monde*, 26 May 1994) showed that more than 18 per cent of adolescents were often violent and as many as 41 per cent occasionally so. While only a small proportion (2.3 per cent) were delinquents (*racketteurs*), more than a third of them were regular drinkers, a fifth were smokers and nearly a quarter used drugs.

In the worldwide market of drugs, explained Giorgio Giacomelli, director of the UN control programme (interviewed by *Le Monde*, 17 June 1997), the big cities offer a particularly favourable environment. 'Social structures, which exercised some control, whether good or bad, have disappeared. The role of the family and religion has diminished and ideologies have disappeared.' But the drug problem, he warned, is not just a menace for individuals but also for governments. 'The legal economy is infiltrated by laundered money that remains under the control of criminals. It is also a threat to political security, because corruption penetrates governments, parliaments and judiciaries.'

Fragmented society

French society is indeed entering a new, unknown world, affirm Henri Mendras and Alistair Cole in their study *Social Change in Modern France*. The great social structures of the nineteenth century are crumbling or have disappeared. The old antagonistic social classes – bourgeoisie, peasants, industrial working class and old middle class – are splitting into a greater number of smaller social groups, most of which form part of a new, central middle-class 'constellation'. Likewise, the formative institutions of the nineteenth century – Church, army, Republic and (secular) school – have lost their symbolic value: they no longer arouse such passion among French people as they used to do (p. 12). Indeed, as the trial in 1997 of the Vichy official Maurice Papon for crimes against humanity has brought out, Pétain's 'national revolution' was the last, vain attempt to assert the most traditional values – army, religion, authority – against modern centrifugal trends.

Now, French society is moving towards the cult of the self, according to marketing studies (appropriately enough!), quoted by Eve Gilliard-Russell, in Perry (ed.) *Aspects of Contemporary France*. This is a narcissistic rather than socially oriented approach to life. 'Individuals are becoming more isolated, withdrawn, they are worried about the future and, when faced with depersonalised consumption (because it is accessible to all), seek their own identity, adopting individualistic, multi-faceted behaviour' (p. 231).

Even the founding values of the welfare state – solidarity, equality and social justice – no longer correspond to the 'all-conquering' values of individualism and economic neo-liberalism, according to Pierre Rosanvallon in *La crise de l'Etat-providence*. The very model of social protection is now at the heart of debate over the role of public expenditure and its effect on economic performance and the creation (or loss) of jobs (Bernadette Galloux-Fournier, *L'Histoire de l'Europe au XXe. siècle*, 110).

Even the legitimacy of the democratic system of political representation is at stake, Rosanvallon argues in a dialogue with Alain Duhamel in *Le Monde* (15–16 January 1995). For 'the political system no longer produces social identification: society has become less "readable", more opaque; it is more and more difficult to be represented'. The reason is not simply the distance between political parties and ordinary people, but 'the fact that the political system no longer understands society; it no longer speaks a language that enables it to understand itself or to perceive its bearings and define its perspectives'. The problem, as Rosanvallon emphasizes, is that politics is not just a function of organizing and rationalizing conflicts but, as a place for creating social ties, it is the realm of symbols and emotion.

In this society of flux and dissolution of traditional bonds – teenage turmoil, women's emancipation, unmarried couples living together, rise in divorce rates, fall of institutional religion (but enthusiasm for 'charismatic' performance), loss of rural roots, identification with image and 'spectacle' – the authority of intellectuals, the very symbol of the French 'exception', is also in decline. Does not the virtual disappearance of intellectuals from public life, suggests Alain Touraine, reveal the fragmentation of society and its values? For the intellectuals, until quite recently, drew their legitimacy from understanding the 'laws of history', which enabled them both to advise modernizing regimes and at the same time to defend the interests of ordinary people.

This role no longer exists. A major reason, argues Touraine, is the 'antimodernist' current of intellectual life, inspired by Nietzsche, and, to some extent, Freud. While this intellectual tendency gains support from 'sociocultural' personalities, teachers and students especially, it no longer reaches the mass of society. For ordinary people spend more time with television than reading; they are aware of their higher standard of living, which allows them to acquire modern household equipment, to have the use of a car, and to go on holidays. This popular culture, spurned by intellectuals for taking a materialist form, according to Touraine, nevertheless signifies the revival of the individual Subject, inspiring emotion, reflection on social relations, and movements of solidarity (*Critique de la modernité*, 461–5).

Solidarity

The notion of social security for everyone is, as Jacques Delors emphasizes, a major form of solidarity. As president of the European Commission from 1985 to 1995, Delors had worked tirelessly to promote the social as well as the economic dimension of the new Europe. Indeed, a nation defines itself by its solidarities, according to Delors: solidarity between generations, between those at work and those outside the work force, between the healthy and the sick. The proportion of national wealth that a country devotes to such efforts of solidarity is vital. Too little solidarity may lead to 'massive exclusion', endangering the economy itself. Excessive solidarity, on the other hand, may produce a dependent society resulting in a loss of economic dynamism (report by Erik Izraelewicz, *Le Monde*, 14 November 1995).

The French programme of social security, like the Beveridge Report in Britain, was elaborated before the end of the Second World War, as if to inaugurate a new, just society on the ruins of the rejected past. Contribution to social insurance was divided between employee (6 per cent) and employer (10 per cent) in France. From the start, social security covered the risks of ill health, invalidity, old age, death and work accidents, while the state was responsible for unemployment benefits (J.-P. Rioux, *La France de la Quatrième République*, vol. 1, 118–19).

Nevertheless, as in Delors' critique of the 'profoundly unjust' and 'ineffective' organization of the social security system, there is a wide gap between the universal principle of solidarity and its particular application, unfairly benefiting some (especially those who are already privileged) and excluding others. Huge protests by medical students in 1982, for example, ended any attempt by the then Socialist government to control the choice of specialists (infringing, for the students, the sacred principle of the patient's freedom of choice) – which was matched more than a decade later by the opposition of most doctors to the Juppé, and then the Jospin, programme of reforms to 'cap' the spiralling costs of the health service. (On the Juppé reforms, see Sabine Ferrand-Nagel in *L'Etat de la France 97–98*, 565–71; on health problems, Pierre Mormiche and others, 143–55.) As Gary Freeman (1994) points out, in his study of social security, governments failed to take into account the power of organized groups to resist egalitarian reforms.

And yet, despite the pessimistic talk of a divided society which has lost its bearings, the analysis by Mendras and Cole leads to an opposite conclusion. They emphasize, in contrast to the failure of state institutions to develop solidarity, the role of voluntary associations, the vitality of local government and the great variety of social allegiances, codes of behaviour and value-systems in contemporary France that do not simply operate in a vacuum. Rather, according to these authors, they form part of an essential consensus over fundamental values (Mendras and Cole, 120–1, 125–9).

Touraine argues along the same lines, except that his 'social movements' contest, rather than coexist with, state power. Moreover, he insists that democracy (popular sovereignty), besides struggling against absolutism, should set limits to 'extreme individualism'. For Touraine, such individualism tends to dissociate civil society from political society, leaving the latter free to indulge in 'corrupt games' or to facilitate the (excessive) power of administrations and enterprises. Democracy, he argues, must combine the integration, or solidarity, of citizens with respect for identities, needs and rights. 'There is no democracy without the combination of an open society and respect for social actors, without the association of cold (rational) procedures and the warmth of conviction and belonging' (Touraine, 417).

But how to reconcile freedom and solidarity? This is the critical question that confronts the nation and its ethnic, and other, minorities. It is a problem that is aggravated by the widespread fear of loss of identity in the new Europe.

National identity

Within France

There are two radically opposed conceptions of French nationality. On the one hand, there is a large political consensus around the historic conception of '*droit du sol*' (the right of children, born in France, to acquire French nationality). But, as Patrick Weil points out in his report on immigration and nationality to the Jospin government, to be born in France of foreign parents is not in itself sufficient. 'It is this [*le sol*], plus residence, plus socialization, that is, education in the society, which produces nationality' (interview, *Le Monde*, 8 August 1997). This is to recall the historic view of assimilation into French civilization.

The opposing view, although politically in the minority (notably Le Pen's National Front), is more deeply rooted in popular opinion: it is the view of those who are uncertain of the future, who fear the effect of change, and who look back nostalgically to a time when France was 'pure' and homogeneous. (A mistaken belief: historically, as is the case with other European countries, immigration has always played an important role.) These diffuse feelings of anxiety, traditionalism and resentment of foreigners ('taking away our jobs' or 'living at the expense of the French') are crystallized in the deliberately racist and polemical utterances of Le Pen, who is well aware that his extreme statements and catchy slogans make good publicity. Moreover, he assumes (not without reason) that what he declares openly many believe in their hearts.

Le Pen's National Front, which sees itself as the only genuine alternative to the established 'corrupt' political parties, offers a catch-all platform to protest-voters, disgruntled traditionalists and the socially and economically deprived. But it is racism that provides the sharpest focus for popular fear and anger; and it is the Muslim Arab communities (and, to a lesser extent, black Africans) that have been singled out as the scapegoat for the crisis in society. (See Stephane Rozès, 'Is France racist?', and Michèle Tribalat on assimilation and immigration figures, *L'Etat de la France 97–98*, 43–5, 69–75.)

'The FN [National Front] says aloud what many of us, activists in the [neo-Gaullist] RPR, think to ourselves', explained one of the delegates at an RPR-sponsored election meeting in south-west France (*Le Monde*, 5 April 1997). 'Our enemy is not the FN', insisted another speaker, declaring that he was 'French 365 days in the year'. Other local supporters of the RPR appealed, echoing the National Front, for a system of 'national preferences' in providing employment (that is, discrimination against foreigners); others suggested that the ten-year resident permit for foreigners should be reduced to three years, while still others sought to exclude immigrants from social service entitlements.

The Jospin government, as by and large its Right-wing predecessor, maintains a 'Republican' stance on immigration. Minister of the Interior Chevènement, for example, while recognizing the serious problem of unemployment in France and 'the profound doubt about its identity and future', nevertheless insisted that

> the identity of France is that of the Republic: a Frenchman or woman is a French citizen, neither more nor less. The citizen-nation is contrary to the ethnic nation. It is defined by a shared project and not by any mythical 'roots'.

It is universal values, he added, that are at the heart of 'modern French patriotism' (interview with *Le Monde*, 26 June 1997).

The problem, of course, is more than a matter of definition. Racist exploitation by the National Front of popular fear and insecurity derives, as J.-M. Colombani, editor of *Le Monde*, rightly states (18 February 1997), from the 'deep crisis of identity of a country which no longer finds its landmarks at this end of the century'. The National Front takes advantage of this 'loss of confidence in democracy, its institutions and political life, in the sincerity of its Republican elites and the effectiveness of its governments'.

Indeed, social malaise is at the heart of the 'tension' between French people and immigrants, according to the three-year study of the High Council on Integration, published in March 1997. Loss of moral standards, weakening of social bonds, family deficiencies, juvenile delinquency: all were identified in the Council's report. On the one hand, there is a 'feeling of insecurity . . . among people belonging to the most fragmented layers of society, who no longer find their collective identity in the nation'. On the other hand, there is the evidence of delinquency, especially among immigrant youth, who suffer from excessively high rates of unemployment (37 per cent of those aged between 15 and 24, or nearly three times the national average). Moreover, prison figures for foreigners increased from 20 per cent of the total in 1980 to 29 per cent in 1996, although foreigners only make up 6.4 per cent of the French population.

Even the schools, supposed bastion of Republican values, were exposed in certain areas to conflicting pressures from those seeking to impose Islamic customs on their children, on the one hand, and those who rejected any kind of 'social mixing' among those of different origins, on the other, according to the Council's report. (See, for example, Inès Brulard, '*Laïcité* and Islam' in S. Perry (ed.) *Aspects of Contemporary France.*)

Within Europe

Immigration, then, is symptomatic of a deeper crisis: that of a people afflicted by unemployment and 'exclusion', worried about insecurity and uncertain of the future. Paradoxically, however, the construction of Europe could itself provide new landmarks and a renewed sense of achievement dispelling the gloomy prognostications of current opinion.

For both hopes and fears about Europe, as Jean Charlot pointed out (1994, 51–2), reflect the internal divisions of French society. Fears express the pessimistic outlook of the less educated and less qualified in the face of modernization, opening to Europe and the world, and hence intensified competition. Hopes, on the other hand, represent the optimistic outlook of the more educated and socially mobile. The main fears are of more unemployment, 'loss of our national identity' and 'too much immigration'. The main hopes are 'more jobs', a more effective competitive stance *vis-à-vis* the

United States and Japan, and the opportunity for work anywhere within Europe.

A way to resolve both the economic and social distress of 'traditionalist' France and to enhance the challenge of the Europeanists or 'modernizers' is proposed in two remarkably converging studies – *Les trente piteuses* by Nicolas Baverez and *Les sept piliers de la réforme* by Roger Godino – coming from authors of different political persuasions: Baverez, a former collaborator of Philippe Séguin, and Godino, associated with Michel Rocard. Thus, on the central issue of employment, both writers urge the abandonment of protectionism so as to concentrate on lowering the costs of production and stimulating the creation of wealth. On the role of the state, both recommend refocusing its expenditure towards youth, infrastructure and investment in new technologies. As for the reform of political institutions, Baverez and Godino agree in advocating a renewable five-year term for the president, more recourse to referendums, an end to the *cumul des mandats*, greater transparency through public evaluation of official projects, and reforms in the education and training of the elites.

Nevertheless, the crucial factor, as Bernard Spitz of the Conseil d'Etat points out in his review of Baverez and Godino (*Le Monde des livres*, 9 January 1998), is that for all the relevance of the two authors' critiques, there is no body of common doctrine in France capable of supporting these much-needed reforms: 'no political force appears ready to sustain the majority of their proposals'. Accordingly, it is up to Baverez and Godino, as it is for all other reformers, in Spitz's opinion, to 'invent' the political conditions that will allow 'organized and renewed forces' in society to endorse their projects. Indeed, the authors, disregarding the established political parties, appeal directly to French citizens – that is, civil society – to do so.

Europe, for Godino, plays a vital role in the modernization of France. Such is also the vision of Jacques Delors in the interview cited above. For Delors, the obsessive fear of the decline of France was what persuaded him to work at the European Commission, so that the Europe of the future, transmitted to his children and grandchildren, would not be crippled or marginalized.

To create a 'powerful and generous' Europe, however, requires distinguishing between the federal and the national spheres. Delors says he had never proposed putting education, culture, social security and health at the European level: these are within a 'strictly national competence'. As for foreign policy and security issues, member countries should indeed act jointly – but only where they have a common interest.

What should properly be dealt with at the European level, as Delors emphasizes – and this is surely the answer to 'nationalist' critics of the

European Union – are precisely those areas where the room for manoeuvre at the national level is no longer sufficient: that is, the economic and monetary fields. This should be self-evident by now. I would like now to conclude by evoking another identity of France, created by observer-participants, who are not French but who love and admire the country and its people. Their 'France' is no less a work of art: the product of reason and imagination.

References

Baverez, N. (1997) *Les trentes piteuses*, Paris: Flammarion.

Brulard, I. (1997) '*Laïcité* and Islam' in S. Perry (ed.) *Aspects of Contemporary France*, London: Routledge.

Charlot, J. (1994) *La politique en France*, Paris: Fallois.

L'Etat de la France 97–98 (1997) Paris: La Découverte.

Le Figaro, 15 September 1997.

Freeman, G. (1994) 'Financial crisis and policy continuity in the Welfare State', in P. Hall, J. Hayward and H. Machin (eds) *Developments in French Politics*, London: Macmillan.

Galloux-Fournier, B. (1995) *L'Histoire de l'Europe au XXe. siècle*, vol. 5, Paris: Complexe.

Gilliard-Russell, E. (1997) 'A market of 58 million consumers' in S. Perry (ed.) *Aspects of Contemporary France*, London: Routledge.

Godino, R. (1997) *Les sept piliers de la réforme*, Paris: Albin Michel.

Mendras, H. and Cole, A. (1991) *Social Change in Modern France*, Cambridge, UK: Cambridge University Press.

Le Monde, various.

Rioux, J.-P. (1980) *La France de la Quatrième République*, vol. 1, Paris: Seuil.

Rosanvallon, P. (1981) *La crise de l'Etat-providence*, Paris: Seuil.

Touraine, A. (1992) *Critique de la modernité*, Paris: Fayard.

Further reading

The French excel in history, sociology and philosophy. As for political writing, there is an impressive heritage: from Jean Bodin (on sovereignty) to Voltaire and Rousseau on the Enlightenment, and Tocqueville on democracy. Contemporary political studies, however, whether by French, British or American scholars, owe much to political science theories developed in the United States.

French historians have made a valuable contribution to the series *Nouvelle histoire de la France contemporaine*, published by Seuil. In particular, S. Berstein, *La France de l'expansion*, vol. 1, and Berstein and J.-P. Rioux, vol. 2, provide perceptive analyses of economy, politics and society during the formative years of the Gaullist Fifth Republic. S. Hazareesingh's *Political Traditions in Modern France* is also an important historical treatment of major political and social issues. M. Winock, *Le Siècle des intellectuels*, engagingly discusses the golden age of French intellectuals from the Dreyfus affair to the 'Age of Sartre', but is thin on the 1980s and 1990s.

P. Bourdieu and A. Touraine are outstanding sociologists, oriented to the Left and Centre, respectively. Bourdieu's studies of French education, elitism (*La Noblesse d'Etat*) and academic life are classics; his notions of cultural and other 'capitals', of 'habitus' and the distorting power of language (*Language and Symbolic Power*) are an integral part of the modern grammar of politics. Touraine, moreover, argues that the rational project of modern society has disintegrated; in his view, free 'social movements' are the only force capable of withstanding the repressive tendencies of political and economic power (Critique de la modernité).

Important studies of French politics have come from American specialists (S. Hoffmann, an editor of *French Politics and Society*, and E. Suleiman, on the elites), by British authors (A. Stevens and V. Wright, both on 'government and politics'; also P. Hall, J. Hayward and H. Machin, editing *Developments in French Politics*) and by noted French academics, such as Jean Charlot, *La politique en France*, and Y. Mény, *La corruption de la République*. In turn, the late F. Furet (a fine historian), J. Julliard and P. Rosanvallon, *La République du Centre*, survey the ideological void of present-day politics, as do H. Mendras and A. Cole, *Social Change in Modern France*. S. Perry's edited *Aspects of Contemporary France* has useful contributions on modern society, from the impact of television to the effect of advertising. Note also the economic and political analyses in the annual *L'Etat de la France*, published by La Découverte, and the journals *French Politics and Society* (Harvard) and especially *Modern and Contemporary France* (Carfax).

In France's rich philosophical-political vein, works by J.-P. Sartre (*Plaidoyer pour les intellectuels*, lectures 2 and 3; also novels, plays and short stories) and S. de Beauvoir (*La Force des choses*, *Les Mandarins*) are outstanding, as are the commentaries of their former friend and later political rival, R. Aron, in *Le Figaro*; see also his fascinating memoir, *Le spectateur engagé*. A. Malraux, de Gaulle's minister of culture, captured the violence of the contemporary world in *L'Espoir* and *La Condition Humaine*, as did A. Camus in *La Peste*, an allegory of defeat (Vichy) and resistance. J. Derrida's 'deconstruction' and, above all, M. Foucault's stimulating *Power/Knowledge* thesis have also profoundly influenced contemporary (if not 'Establishment') political and sociological thinking.

Index